Nostradamus, the Great Quatrains, and Symbolism

Nostradamus' use of Symbolism
to express Mystical Ideas
of Future Events

Ken Bist

Copyright © 2015 K. Bist
All rights reserved.
ISBN: 9798599778639

DEDICATION

This book is dedicated to my wife Ronda, for her wonderful support over many years and to my children Jessica, Jennifer, Jordan, and Grandson Darius

Thank you

CONTENTS

Section One:

1. How do we define Symbolism   1

2. Why Symbols are Essential to the Great Quatrains   2

3. Symbols and Images   3

4. Symbols and Emotion   5

5. Symbols and Phonetics   5

6. Symbols and Dialectic   5

Section Two:

1. Nostradamus' Use of Symbolism in WW 3   6

2. Nostradamus' Use of Symbolism in WW 2   8

3. Nostradamus' Use of Symbolism in WW 1   10

4. Nostradamus' Use of Symbolism with Napoleon   11

Section Three

1. Symbolism and the Great Flood   12

2. Symbolism and the Great Famine   13

3. Symbolism and 911   14

Section Four

1. List of Great Quatrains that Demonstrate
   the Use of Symbolism   15

2. Great Quatrains Interpretations
   Showing Symbolism   22

   Great Quatrains and World War 3
   with Symbolism   24

   Great Quatrains and World War 2
   with Symbolism   153

   Great Quatrains and World War 1
   with Symbolism   189

3. Glossary of Symbols   195

Section 1

1. How do we define Symbolism

To Nostradamus a symbol is not simply a thing
to represent other things. To Nostradamus a symbol
is imbued with self consciousness of a future event,
always meaning much more than it represents.
The symbol has an existential aspect that
captures the meaning of future events in there
totality. Implied in the symbol for Nostradamus,
is a biblical exegesis of scripture that captures
the essence.

A symbol is a sign or mark representing an idea,
which creates future connections between different
concepts, and between different time periods.

Thus, symbols are images that carry more than
mere information. They are also the carriers of the
possibility of future events. They express what
Nostradamus couldn't say or express,
and yet they capture the
moment perfectly.

2. Why Symbols are Essential to the Great Quatrains.

That Nostradamus used many symbols
in his <u>Les Prophecies</u> is understandable. This
is because he was viewing future events, to which
there were no preceding cause and effect to help
make these future events understandable.
While the events he was seeing were true events,
he needed symbols to express these future
events and give them a body and soul.

Nostradamus knew that symbols can
stretch across time periods, and would serve
him well in expressing future events.
This is important because for Nostradamus
he is using symbols, to replace words that have
not yet been created. For example, the word
Submarine did not exist when he wrote
<u>Les Prophecies</u>, hence he uses the
symbol of an Iron Fish.

3. Symbols and Images

One of the first symbol images that Nostradamus uses is that of a Fishing Boat, in Great Quatrain 1, which is an ancient symbol for Christianity. Here we see this symbol stretching across time and space, to bring a quick understanding of events surrounding the 911 attacks.

However, he also uses future type symbols to express an understanding with a future generation. What comes to mind is the image of President Bush with a bull horn standing on the rubble of the twin towers with the wings of airplanes at his feet. This is an iconic symbol that we all know, or at least the generation that experienced 911 knows. Nostradamus uses this future symbol while creating his first Great Quatrain 1.

Throughout <u>Les Prophecies</u> Nostradamus uses symbolic images to represent countries. The *Wild Boar* for Germany, the *Eagle* for the United States, the *Lion or Great Lion* for the United Kingdom, and *The Cock* for France. China is represented by the *Moon* and the *Sun* for Japan.

Nostradamus also uses images of colours
to symbolise countries. These colours bear
a striking resemblance to the flags of countries.
For example, he calls Russia the *Red One*.
For the United States he calls it the *Red
and White*, similar to the stripes
on an American Flag.

Nostradamus uses the Pillar of Porphyry,
for a nuclear blast cloud. Darts from Heaven are
missiles. The coalition between Russia and China
he says *is born with two heads and four arms*,
and will last for a few years. This is the coalition
that occurs just before World War 3. Finally,
Nostradamus uses the Great Venice
to represent the European
Union, meaning a large
trading centre.

4. Symbols and Emotion

The best example of symbols and emotion is the description of the Pearl Harbour attack by the Japanese. Nostradamus describes it as *The Stinking and Abominable Defiling that was Successful,* in Great Quatrain 148. Here we see symbolism and emotion, used to describe an event that was both abhorrent for the U.S., and yet successful for the Japanese.

5. Symbols and Phonetics

For example, Nostradamus uses the words *Androgen Born*, which is clearly an attempt at making a phonetic interpretation of the words hydrogen bomb.

6. Symbols and Dialectic

If we look at the metaphysics of a dialectical process, hence transcending the immediate time and space for a future time and space, we can see that the second moment of a future prediction posits a third moment which encompasses the first two predictions. During the Great Quatrain 148 on Midway, Nostradamus states that, *Wasps and bees shall make much of him mad (Nagumo), For being treacherous cup bearers and poisoning the cup.* In other words, the Japanese were defeated at Midway because of the emotional impact caused by Pearl Harbour in the first instant.

Section Two

1. Nostradamus' Symbolism and WW 3

WW 3 (World War 3) is rich in symbolism. This is not only because World War 3 has many more Great Quatrains associated with it, but also because Nostradamus considered it the most important event in world history. This may be inferred from his vision of that event. The complex series of national and international events that he describes will lead to the death of billions of people.

That Nostradamus considers WW 3 to be the most important event in world history, can also be inferred by the large number of Great Quatrains that he devotes to this one event. In total there are 181 Great Quatrains devoted to this one event out of a potential of 250 Great Quatrains. In other words, over 72% of all Great Quatrains are devoted to describing WW 3.

According to Nostradamus WW 3 starts on New Years Day 2025. Nostradamus predicts that the war will last seven months in total, until the end of July 2025.

Nostradamus also explains his understanding of religious symbols in WW 3. Symbols like the Beast, and the number 666 from Revelations are described as the hydrogen bomb, and the three waves of 607 missiles that Russia attacks North America with during WW 3.

To Nostradamus the term *Clergy* simply means leadership, which he uses several times, during WW 3.

Even relatively simple symbols like the term Horse means something else to Nostradamus. The term *Horse,* which he uses many times throughout the Great Quatrains, is a symbol for a Boat.

In World War 3 Nostradamus describes the U.S. Navy as the "Proud Neptune".

The Dali Lama is safe in a *Barn on the Sea.*
This is how Nostradamus describes
an Aircraft carrier, as a barn
on the sea.

Submarines he calls
an *Iron Fish.*

A nuclear blast on the sea
is *A Sun Upon the Sea.*

2. Nostradamus' Symbolism and WW 2

Nostradamus when presenting the Great Quatrains and WW 2, manages to capture the essence.

He calls Hitler the Anti-Christ, and the rise of fascism he calls *a movement with heart, feet, hands and sense*. Describing fascism as an ascetic movement is an excellent way of putting it. Fascism he states is a new sect of Philosophers that shall arise, despising death, gold, honors or riches. They are *Idiots without Heads* means fascism lacks intelligence and consciousness.

When describing the pincer movement of German tanks in WW 2, Nostradamus says they are *Two evils of a scorpion joined*.

The swastika he calls either the *mobile sign* or the *broken cross*.

German submarines are *the concealed evil*.

During the Warsaw Ghetto Uprising Nostradamus predicts the Germans will be *repulsed with bows, fires and pitch*.

That everyone shall shelter under *the Great Line*,
means those in London in WW 2 will shelter
in the Tube.

During the Normandy invasion of WW 2,
all aircraft were painted with stripes on the
wings similar to hornets. Nostradamus
calls them *Hornets flying low*,
to strafe German positions.

3. Nostradamus' Symbolism and WW 1

Nostradamus calls WW 1 the Great War,
and this is what writers at the time said about WW 1.
They called it the Great War to End all Wars.

Nostradamus says *the sky that was serene
shall show sword and lance* predicting the introduction
of the Air War in WW 1.

The *Lion and the Cock* shall not agree very well
predicts that England and France will not work
well together during WW 1, but *for fear shall
help one another.*

On the *left hand the affliction shall be greater*,
meaning the Western Front during WW 1
will suffer the most.

He predicts the symbol of a *Gray Bird, holding
a green bough.* Here Nostradamus is predicting
the peace offering from England's diplomat
Sir Edward Grey.

Then a great one will die and the war be finished,
is a reference to the death of Emperor Francis
Joseph of Austria. Once he died the war
quickly came to an end.

4. Nostradamus' Symbolism and Napoleon

According to Nostradamus Napoleon came
to power under the feigned shadow of freeing people
from slavery. He shall usurp the people and city
for himself, meaning he will take over Paris
and France under this false pretext.

Nostradamus says that this *concavity*
or downward trend with Napoleon, was held
in place by *marble and metallic lead*. By this
he means that Napoleon maintained power because
of the illusion of marble palaces, and lead,
meaning bullets and cannon.

Napoleon says Nostradamus will go from a King
to a *Pacific Emperor*, which happened when
Napoleon crowned himself Emperor in 1804.

Napoleon will die when *a burning sun shall
pour into the throat.* Nostradamus is predicting
Napoleon's death from water poisoning from a well.
Nostradamus says that Napoleon *shall be drowned
in a well.* The symbol of a well for Napoleon
comes from Napoleons father, as it was believed
that his father drowned his first two children
in a well. Napoleon was also defeated by a well,
in the form of the Duke of Wellington. Also,
Napoleon's final resting place is a well like structure,
with his sarcophagus at the centre of the well
and his victories and statues surrounding
him at Les Invalides in Paris.

Section Three

1. Symbolism and the Great Flood

In Great Quatrain 227 Nostradamus predicts
that for 40 years prior to WW 3 *the rainbow shall
not appear*. He is referring to global warming prior
to the war. But after the war *for 40 years
the rainbow shall appear every day*
implies a great flood.

The world-wide flood is caused by the
destruction of the north and south poles.

The waters threaten another *Deucalion*,
says Nostradamus. He is implying a worldwide
flood similar to the times of Noah.

The year following being discovered by a flood
meaning the year following WW 3.

2. Symbolism and the Great Famine

In Great Quatrain 17 and Great Quatrain 250 Nostradamus predicts a worldwide famine after WW 3.

Manna shall no more fall, states the destruction of the food chain.

The great famine do I see drawing near, Turning from one way to another and then becoming universal, so great and long, that they shall come to pluck, the root from the wood and the child from the breast.

Although the Great Famine will start during WW 3, it will eventually become universal after the war.

So great a famine with a plague implies radiation is the cause of the famine.

3. Symbolism and 911

Taken Captive Above Four Times states
Nostradamus in Great Quatrain 150.
During 911 four planes were hijacked above.

The heaven shall burn at five and forty
degrees, the fire shall come near the great new city,
In an instant a great flame dispersed shall burst out,
When they shall make a trial of the Normans.

In New York city, the great new city, there
will be a fire the instant a plane hits the tower
on a forty-five-degree angle. At that time the
Normans, or Americans, will be tested.

Where to the heavens is seen the amphitheatre,
meaning there are events taking place in the sky
worth watching. Everyone is watching the sky
clear of planes.

A List of all the Great Quatrains Dealing with Symbolism

List of Great Quatrains and World War 3
with Symbolism

Great Quatrain 1	The 911 Attacks The International Debate	24
Great Quatrain 2	World War 3 14 Syrian Terrorists	27
Great Quatrain 4	World War 3 Exile Ships at Marseille 70 Nuclear Explosions	30
Great Quatrain 5	World War 3 Mini-subs with Nuclear Weapons	33
Great Quatrain 11	The Soviet Union The Hydrogen Bomb Andrei Sakharov	36
Great Quatrain 14	World War 3 Two Heads and Four Arms Russia and China	39
Great Quatrain 16	World War 3 The Beast Speaks	42

Great Quatrain 17	World War 3 The Great Famine The Great Mountain	45
Great Quatrain 20	World War 3 Nine Nuclear Nations	48
Great Quatrain 21	World War 3 Woman Chinese Premiere	51
Great Quatrain 38	World War 3 Two Great Wrestlers	54
Great Quatrain 39	World War 3 The Crown	57
Great Quatrain 40	World War 3 Aircraft Carrier Sunk	59
Great Quatrain 43	World War 3 Darts from Heaven	62
Great Quatrain 46	World War 3 The Great Flood	64
Great Quatrain 49	World War 3 Cities Deserted	67
Great Quatrain 54	World War 3 The Ark	70
Great Quatrain 60	World War 3 United States and NATO Wins Air War	73

Great Quatrain 64	World War 3 607 Missiles in Three Waves	76
Great Quatrain 78	World War 3 The 12 Red Ones	79
Great Quatrain 88	World War 3 The Guillotine Returns	82
Great Quatrain 94	World War 3 The White Country	85
Great Quatrain 103	World War 3 The Solar Ship	88
Great Quatrain 110	World War 3 The Three Hundred	90
Great Quatrain 116	World War 3 Trident Taken	92
Great Quatrain 120	World War 3 The Great Ogmion	94
Great Quatrain 121	World War 3 The Eastern Wall Falls	96
Great Quatrain 128	World War 3 The Temple of Colours	99
Great Quatrain 131	World War 3 Fear in the East	102

Great Quatrain 132	World War 3 The Great Emperor Henry The Roman Emperor Putin	105
Great Quatrain 134	World War 3 ALUS	108
Great Quatrain 143	World War 3 Henry the Victor	110
Great Quatrain 145	World War 3 Romans Claim Eagle	113
Great Quatrain 150	911 Attacks Taken Captive Above	116
Great Quatrain 186	World War 3 A Fox	119
Great Quatrain 203	World War 3 New Clay	122
Great Quatrain 207	World War 3 The Great Cap	125
Great Quatrain 208	World War 3 Column of Porphyry	127

Great Quatrain 223	World War 3 The Young Ogmion	130
Great Quatrain 227	World War 3 Deucalion Again	133
Great Quatrain 231	World War 3 A Barrel of Honey	136
Great Quatrain 236	World War 3 Shadow of the Seven	138
Great Quatrain 242	World War 3 An Earthquake in May	141
Great Quatrain 243	President Putin 666 is the number of a man	144
Great Quatrain 249	World War 3 A and A	148
Great Quatrain 250	World War 3 Manna Shall No More Fall	150

List of Great Quatrains and World War 2 with Symbolism

Great Quatrain 8	World War 2 Bridge too Far	153
Great Quatrain 13	World War 2 Events Leading Up	156
Great Quatrain 45	World War 2 War Crimes	159
Great Quatrain 50	World War 2 D-Day	162
Great Quatrain 59	World War 2 Hitler Stroke	165
Great Quatrain 87	World War 2 Hornets	168
Great Quatrain 111	World War 2 Double Army	171
Great Quatrain 135	World War 2 Holocaust	174
Great Quatrain 148	World War 2 Midway	177
Great Quatrain 190	World War 2 Twice Set Up	180
Great Quatrain 195	World War 2 Anti-Christ	183

Great Quatrain 248	World War 2 Ropes and Rushes	186

List of Great Quatrains and World War 1 with Symbolism

Great Quatrain 23	World War 1 The Great War	189
Great Quatrain 25	World War 1 The Gray Bird	193

Great Quatrains and World War 3 with Symbolism

Important Symbols to know prior to reading
the interpretations.

The Beast -   The hydrogen bomb

Pillar of Porphyry -   A nuclear blast cloud

Exiles -

The vast majority of the Exiles are Arabs from the Middle East. Many of those who are coming back from Russia, are disgraced. There are Russian troops hidden among them. They are well aware of the timing and location of the nuclear explosions from the mini-subs in Europe, although they claim not to be connected with these terrorists. While the route they take in France appears meandering, it was in fact decided upon long ago. They are arriving in Europe with the Russian Chinese flotilla. There are no flags on any of the flotilla ships. They enter France carrying signs saying:
We come in Peace.

Twelve Red One's -

Terrorists recruited by Russia to pilot mini-subs with nuclear weapons into European Ports, or to attack America and American ships and naval facilities. They target the most important international ports in Europe, and the United States. They come from Syria and the Beqaa Valley, where Russia recruited them in 2015.

Barbarians -

These are Barbarian hordes of people from Russia, China, and the Middle East, following the Russian Chinese Joint Military. They are made up of a group of churls. There are terrorists hidden among them. Some, but very few, include Exiles for Hungary, Austria, Germany, and Italy. The Barbarian horde that is moving through Romania and Hungary is very large. They arrive in Europe by land. There are Russian troops hidden among them. They will claim to be refugees, needing Russian military protection.

Terrorists -

Made up of Arabs from Syria and the Middle East. Some are trained to use a Russian mini-sub, with a nuclear weapon. Others are part of the Barbarians from Iran. Nostradamus calls them the sons of Hama or Hamas.

Ogmion -

These are the NATO military leaders in Europe. The first one is killed at the start of World War 3. The second one will place his ensigns at the end of the war, so people know civilization has returned.

Great Quatrain 1

(Century I 3/ Century I 4/Century I 5/Century I 6)

Interpretation:

The 911 Attacks
The International Debate

Summary:

With the 911 Attacks there is an international debate on state terrorism. People cover their faces, and run from the collapse of the World Trade Centre. A new administration in the United States is elected. The tower or towers are predicted to be rebuilt after their destruction.

Century I 3

When the litter shall be overthrown, by a gust of wind,
And faces shall be covered with cloaks,
The Republic shall be vexed by new people,
Then shall White and Red judge wrongly.

The litter with gusts of wind and dust, describes the events immediately following the destruction of the twin towers. People running from the destruction are seen covering their faces with their coats. The Republic vexed by new people, informs us of the new administration in the White House, under President George W. Bush. *White and red*, is one of the terms that Nostradamus uses for the United States, and *judge wrongly* refers to Iraq.

Century I 4

In the world shall be a Monarch,
Who will not leave peace, nor be long alive,
Then will be lost the Fishing Boat,
And shall be governed to its great detriment.

In the world shall be a monarch refers to Bin Laden.
Who will not leave peace, nor be long alive, reveals that he won't bring peace and won't live long. *Then will be lost the fishing boat*, suggesting that Christianity has lost its way, due to militant Islam. *Governed to its grief and detriment*, such that the world will face great injury.

Century I 5

They shall be driven away without great fight,
Those of the country shall be greatly grieved,
Town and City shall have a mighty debate,
Carcassonne, Narbonne shall prove their heart.

Those driven away are the terrorists in Afghanistan, responsible for the 911 Attack, leaving the cities with no resistance. In the United States, people will be *greatly grieved* to see them flee.

Town and city shall have a mighty debate, as the public discusses the 911 Attacks, terrorism generally, and state terrorism. *Carcassonne, Narbonne shall prove their heart*, states that these towns, located around a future terrorist attack, will prove they are up to the task as would be Boston and Washington around New York, for example.

Century I 6

The eye of Ravenna shall be destitute,
When the wings shall rise at his feet,
The two of Brescia shall have established Turin and Venice,
Which the French shall have trod upon.

The eye of Ravenna is Bin Laden, who foresees the 911 Attacks and remains *destitute*, despite trying to make money off the attacks through the stock market. *When the wings shall rise at his feet*, is President George W. Bush predicting that the towers, or tower, will be rebuilt. The *two of Brescia*, or the twin towers, is similar to Brescia Italy, which will be at the center of a future terrorist attack. Turin and Venice are just outside the damaged area, like Boston and Washington. *Which the French shall have trod upon*, refers to the Statue of Liberty, and the French involvement in helping the new Republic of the United States establish itself.

Great Quatrain 2

(Century I 7/Century I 8/Century I 9/Century I 10)

Interpretation:

World War 3
14 Syrian Terrorists

Summary:

Russia in the year 2015, chooses 14 Syrian terrorists from the Beqaa Valley, for a Mini-sub nuclear weapons mission. These terrorists will attack European Ports during World War 3. At the start of World War 3, Marseille and Malta are attacked by this method.

Century I 7

One arriving too late, the execution will take place,
The wind being contrary, and letters intercepted on the way,
The conspirators fourteen of a separate body,
By the Red One, the enterprise shall be undertaken.

One arriving too late, the execution will take place, infers that the plan has already been executed. *The wind being contrary and letters intercepted,* reveals luck has changed to the negative, causing the interception of compromising messages. *The conspirators fourteen of a separate body,* implies there will be fourteen terrorists committed to a special task.

By the red one, the enterprise shall be undertaken, infers that Russia will be behind this terrorist attack. Nostradamus uses the term *red one*, for Russia.

Century I 8

How often taken, O city of the Sun shall thou be?
Changing thy vain and barbarous laws,
Thy Evil growth nigh, thou shalt be more tributary,
The great Venice shall recover thy veins.

How often taken, O city of the sun, is Heliopolis or Baalbek near Damascus in the Beqaa Valley. It is here that terrorists will begin their evil plot. *Thy evil growth nigh, thou shalt be more tributary*, tells us that evil will spread out from Baalbek. The *great Venice,* or the trading nations that make up the European Union, will discover where this evil has come from.

Century I 9

From the East of Africa shall come the Lion-Heart,
To vex Venice and the heirs of Romulus,
Accompanied by the Libyan Tribe,
Malta shall tremble and the neighbouring
islands shall be empty.

From the east of Africa shall come the lion-heart, the terrorist leader of this group. He shall cause Venice, or the European Union, and the *heirs of Romulus,* the United States, to be concerned.

Accompanied by the Libyan tribe or other terrorists,
causing Malta and the neighbouring islands to empty.

Century I 10

Sergeants sent into the Cage of Iron,
Where the seven children of the King are,
The old men and fathers shall see the death and cries
of their first fruit,
And before they die, shall go through Hell.

Sergeants sent into the cage of iron, are surgeons
or physicians sent into radiation proof areas, to help those
in need. Fathers will witness their children harmed from the
explosion and the radiation fallout, going *through hell*
and turmoil *before they die.*

Great Quatrain 4

(Century I 15/Century I 16/Century I 17/Century I 18)

Interpretation:

World War 3
Exile Ships at Marseille
70 Nuclear Explosions

Summary:

Exile ships at Marseille will come from Russia. They are turned away from Marseille, and disembark at Barcelona. The Third World War will cause 70 nuclear explosions, near or on populated areas. This will lead people to no longer trust their political leaders. Many will die due to the changing environmental conditions, such as radiation poisoning, and a rise in sea levels around the globe.

Century I 15

Mars threatens us with a warlike force,
Seventy times he shall cause blood to be shed,
Causing the ruin of the Clergy,
And those who will hear nothing from them.

Seventy times he shall cause blood to be shed, explains that during World War 3, there will be 70 nuclear explosions that will hit near or on populated areas. *Causing the ruin of the clergy,* or in other words, causing people to mistrust their leaders.

And those who will hear nothing from them, implies
they won't listen to anything they have to say either.

Century I 16

When a fish pond that was a meadow shall be mowed,
Sagittarius being in the ascendant,
Plague, Famine, Death by the military hand,
The Century approaches renewal.

When a fish pond shall be mowed, states that small bodies
of water will dry up, because the earth's atmosphere has changed.
Sagittarius being in the ascent, tells us that World War 3 will
begin to take shape between Nov.22 and Dec.22. *Plague, famine,*
death by the military hand, infers that the changes will come about
as a result of war. *The century approaches renewal*, states that
after World War 3 and after these environmental changes,
close to the new century in the year 2100, there will
be a period of renewal.

Century I 17

For forty years the rainbow shall not appear,
For forty years it shall be seen every day,
The parched earth shall wax drier and drier,
And a great flood when it shall appear.

For forty years the rainbow shall not appear,
informs us that global warming will continue for forty
years, prior to World War 3. *The parched earth*
shall wax drier and drier, in other words.

However, after World War 3, *the rainbow shall be seen everyday*, describes a global flood, causing a rainbow to appear every day.

Century I 18

Through the discord and negligence of the French,
A passage shall be opened to Mahomet,
The land and sea of Italy shall be bloody,
And the harbour of Marseilles shall be
covered with sails and ships.

Part of the reason for the devastating effects of World War 3, is that France is *negligent* to the warnings it receives. Because of this negligence, *a passage is open to Mahomet*, tells us that terrorists will take advantage of this negligence. *The land and sea of Italy shall be bloody*, informs us about battles in and around Italy. *And the harbour of Marseille shall be covered with sails and ships,* says that there are many ships near Marseille, bringing the Exile people from Russia into this region.

Great Quatrain 5

(Century I 19/Century I 20/Century I 21/Century I 22)

Interpretation:

World War 3
Mini-subs with nuclear weapons

Summary:

There are Mini-subs with nuclear weapons, in the rivers of France. Russia will not allow NATO to fly over the Exile ships at Marseille, and will provide their own air cover. At this time, terrorists from Spain will enter France. The President of France, will hide among the people fleeing Paris. The nuclear explosions within France, will overload the assistance capacity of some French cities. Terrorists will not claim any responsibility after the explosions.

Century I 19

When the serpents shall come to encompass the air,
The French blood shall be angered by Spain,
By them, a great number shall perish,
The chief flies, and hides in the rushes of the marshes.

When the serpents shall come to encompass the air, states that Russia provides air cover to the Exile ships near Marseille, and won't allow NATO to control the airspace above Marseille and this region.

The French shall *be angered by Spain* because *by them,
a great number shall perish*, implies that some of the terrorists
will enter from Spain, and are Spanish in origin. *The chief flies,
and hides in the rushes of the marshes,* suggests that the
President of France, will hide among the
people that are fleeing Paris.

Century I 20

*Tours, Orleans, Blois, Angers, Reims and Nantes,
Cities vexed by sudden change,
By strange languages tents shall be set up,
Rivers, Darts, Rennes, Land and Sea shall tremble.*

Tours, Orleans, Blois, Angers, Reims and Nantes,
are cities vexed by sudden change because they are
on the edges of the nuclear blasts. They find it difficult
to help people fleeing, as their assistance capacity
is overloaded. *By strange languages tents shall be set up*,
reveals that the Exile people flowing into France from the
south, will set up multilingual tents along the way, to rally
support to their cause. They are selling utopia. *Rivers, darts,
Rennes, land and sea shall tremble* states that the dart,
or mini-sub with a nuclear weapon, is in the rivers,
causing the earth and sea to shake like an earthquake
near Rennes.

Century I 21

*A deep white clay a rock supports,
Which shall break out of the deep like milk,
In vain people shall be troubled not daring to touch it,
Being ignorant that in the bottom there is a milky clay.*

A deep white clay a rock supports, which shall break out of the deep like milk, is the image of white fallout material from a nuclear blast. *In vain people shall be troubled not daring to touch it*, implies that people will still touch the white fallout, even though they know they shouldn't. *Being ignorant that in the bottom there is a milky clay*, tells us that people are unaware that in the blast area, covered with water, there is a radioactive material that can kill them.

Century I 22

That which shall live shall leave no direction,
Its destruction and death will come by stratagem,
Auton, Chalons, Langres, and both sides,
The war and ice shall do great harm.

That which shall live shall leave no direction, suggests that terrorists will leave no message taking responsibility. *Its destruction and death will come by stratagem*, shows that there was significant long-range planning in these acts of terrorism. *Auton, Chalons, Langres, and from both sides* states that these towns just outside the blast areas, will experience the negative environmental impact from both sides. Radiation from the Marseille blast, as well as radiation from the Rouen and Chartres blasts near Paris. *The war and ice shall do great harm* implies that war, and negative environmental changes together will cause many deaths.

Great Quatrain 11

(Century I 43/Century I 44/Century I 45/Century I 46)

Interpretation:

The Soviet Union
The Hydrogen Bomb
Andrei Sakharov

Summary:

The inventor of the Hydrogen Bomb, Andrei Sakharov will become famous. The Hydrogen Bomb will be used in World War 3. The Soviet Union will test a Hydrogen Bomb in the Arctic Circle. An arms race will ensue, with both sides making personal sacrifices.

Century I 43

Before the change in Empire comes,
There shall be a strange accident,
A field shall be changed, and a pillar of Porphyry,
Shall be transported upon the chalky cliffs.

Before the change of empire comes, or before the Soviet Union collapses, and introduces glasnost and perestroika, *there shall be a strange accident, a field shall be changed, and a pillar of porphyry, shall be transported upon the chalky cliffs.*

The pillar of porphyry, is Nostradamus' term for a nuclear blast cloud. In 1961 the Soviet Union tested a 50 megaton Hydrogen Bomb in the Arctic Circle, on the white mountains of an Arctic Archipelago.

Century I 44

In a short time, sacrifices shall return again,
Opposers shall be put to martyrdom,
There shall no more monks, abbots, nor novices,
Honey shall be dearer than wax.

In a short time, sacrifices shall return again, implies that the nuclear race between the United States and Russia will involve personal sacrifice. *Opposers shall be put to martyrdom*, is suggesting that those who are in opposition to the Soviet Union's development of nuclear weapons, those who dissent, will be sacrificed. *There shall be no more monks, abbots, nor novices*, tells us that the Russians will not make a distinction between rank, intelligence, class, or person, in their desire to obtain the Hydrogen Bomb at any cost. *Honey shall be dearer than wax*, infers that for the average Russian in this period of austerity, food will be more important than luxury goods.

Century I 45

Followers of Sects, great pains to the informer,
A beast on the stage prepares the scenes,
The inventor of that iniquitous fact shall be famous,
By sects the world shall be confused and schismatic.

Followers of sects, great pains to the informer, explains
that those who divulge secrets to the enemy during this
period will suffer. *Followers of sects*, like capitalism
or communism, will suffer great pains, if they divulge
secrets of the hydrogen bomb. *A beast on the stage prepares
the scenes*, describes the Russians as they get ready
to demonstrate a 50-megaton nuclear blast for the United
States. Nostradamus uses the term beast to describe the
hydrogen bomb. *The inventor of that iniquitous fact shall
be famous* refers to Andrei Sakharov, and his creation
of the Hydrogen Bomb in 1961. After building the H-bomb,
Sakharov went on to denounce it, and then became
an advocate for civil rights within Russia. He eventually
won a Nobel Peace Prize in 1975, for his struggles to bring
civil rights to Russia, for which he faced state persecution.
By sects the world shall be confused and schismatic,
infers that these sects, like capitalism and communism,
will cause confusion and division in the world.

Century I 46

Near Auch, Lectoure and Mirande,
A great fire shall from the sky for three nights fall,
A thing shall happen stupendous and Wonderful,
And shortly after the ground shall shake.

Near Auch, Lectoure and Mirande, a great fire from the sky
for three days shall fall, describes a Hydrogen Bomb that falls
close to these towns in World War 3, causing a great fire
in the sky for three days. *A thing shall happen stupendous*
and wonderful, and shortly after, the explosion will
cause an earthquake, and people will
be in shock from the blast.

Great Quatrain 14

(Century I 55/Century I 56/Century I 57/Century I 58)

Interpretation:

World War 3
Two Heads and Four Arms
Russia and China

Summary

Two heads and four arms, describes Russia and China
forming a Joint Military Structure, which will last a few years.
Blood will be spilled in the North Pole, as well as the South Pole,
in World War 3. China will be led by a Women Premier.
Japan will have a nuclear explosion, at the mouth
of a river on the northern side of the main island.
The United States will provide
assistance to Japan.

Century I 55

In the climate opposite to the Babylonian,
There shall be a great effusion of blood,
So that the land and sea, air and heaven shall seem unjust,
Sects and famine shall rule over plague and confusion.

In the climate opposite to the Babylonian, there shall be a great effusion of blood, states that in the cold climate of the North Pole and the South Pole, there will be explosions on the ice, sea, and in the air, causing blood to be spilled.

So that the land, and sea, air and heaven shall seem unjust, suggests that while war rages, people around the world will be praying for peace. Even *heaven* or space will be a battlefield. *Sects and famine shall rule over plague and confusion,* tells us that political and military divisions, along with a general shortage of food during World War 3, will take precedence, or be of more concern, than radiation sickness and war.

Century I 56

Sooner or later, you shall see great changes,
Extreme horrors and persecutions,
The moon led by an angel,
The heaven draws near its inclination.

People will be persecuted during World War 3 with *horrors*. *The moon led by her angel*, explains that China will be led by a Woman Premier. *The heaven draws near its inclination*, tells us that the United States will use speed to conquer space in World War 3.

Century I 57

By great discord, the trumpet shall vibrate,
Agreement broken, lifting the head to heaven,
A bloody mouth shall swim in blood,
The face turned to the sun, anointed with milk and honey.

At the start of World War 3, Russia and China will break international agreements, and the West will go on a military footing as a result.

People around the world will pray to heaven for peace. *A bloody mouth shall swim in blood, the face turned to the sun, anointed with milk and honey,* states that at the mouth of a river in Japan, there will be a nuclear explosion causing much damage and death. The United States will provide assistance for Japan, with relief efforts and supplies.

Century I 58

Slit in the belly, it shall be born with two heads,
And four arms, shall live a few years,
The day that Aquila shall celebrate his feasts,
Fossan, Turin, the chief of Ferrara shall run away.

Slit in the belly, it shall be born with two heads, and four arms, and live a few years, suggests that both the Russian and Chinese military will form a Joint Military Structure, which will look very unnatural and last only for a few years leading up to World War 3. *Fossan, Turin, the chief of Ferrara shall run away,* tells us that there is a nuclear explosion in Northern Italy, with the cities of Fossan, Turin, and Ferrara, just outside the blast site.

Great Quatrain 16

(Century I 63/Century I 64/Century I 65/Century I 66)

Interpretation:

World War 3
The Beast Speaks

Summary:

The beast speaks, is Nostradamus' way of saying, a nuclear explosion. After World War 2, there will be a period of prosperity and safety. However, this will end with the 911 Attacks, and then the wars will begin anew. There will be air battles around nuclear blast clouds, in World War 3, and lasers will be introduced. The Royal child Prince George, will be wounded by lasers.

Century I 63

The scourge being past, the world shall be made smaller,
Peace for a long time, lands inhabited,
Everyone safe shall go by air, land and sea,
And then the wars shall begin anew.

The scourge being past, the world shall be made smaller, states that after World War 2 or *the scourge,* the world will *be made smaller* with technological advances. *Peace for a long time, lands inhabited, everyone safe shall go by air, land, and sea*, describes the period after World War 2, and the decades of peace that followed.

And then the wars shall begin again, implies the present age, with wars starting over after the 911 Attacks.

Century I 64

They shall think to have seen the sun in the night,
When the hog half a man shall be seen,
Noise, singing, battles in the sky shall be perceived,
And brute beasts shall be heard to speak.

They shall think to have seen the sun in the night, when the hog half a man shall be seen, suggests that there will be nuclear explosions in the night, lighting up the sky. Fighter pilots will be at high altitude, around the explosion. *Noise, singing, battles in the sky shall be perceived*, states there will be air wars between NATO and Russia, near the explosions. *And brute beasts shall be heard to speak,* tells us that there will be more nuclear explosions to come.

Century I 65

A child without hands, lightning never so great was seen,
The Royal child, wounded at the tennis court,
Bruised at the well, lightning going to the ground,
Three in the midst of the field shall be struck thereby.

A child without hands, lightening never so great was seen, The Royal child, wounded at the tennis court, bruised at the well, lightning going to the ground, states that a Royal child from London, Prince George, will be at the tennis court in Falkland Scotland, and shall sustain wounds during the war.

Three in the midst of the field, shall be struck thereby, are the others with Prince George, who are also injured by laser weapons which make their appearance in World War 3.

Century I 66

He that then shall carry the news,
A little while after shall draw his breath,
Viviers, Tournon, Montserrat, and Pradelles,
Hail and storm shall make them sigh.

He that then shall carry the news, a little while after shall draw his breath, refers to the United States Military leader and NATO leader, who will draw his breath at explaining the beginning of World War 3 to Europe and the World. *Viviers, Tournon, Montserrat, and Pradelles, hail and storm shall make them sigh,* tells us that each of these *cities* will experience the effects of the nuclear explosions in their own vicinity, with large deadly hail occurring.

Great Quatrain 17

(Century I 67/Century I 68/Century I 69/Century I 70)

Interpretation:

World War 3
The Great Famine
The Great Mountain

Summary:

A Great Famine will occur a few years after the end,
of World War 3. The famine will be universal across the globe,
because the radiation in the air has entered the earth, making the
soil sterile. Shortly afterwards the Chinese economy will fail,
bringing down individuals, corporations, and even countries.
Three innocents will be charged, with the poisoning
of President Putin of Russia.

Century I 67

The great famine do I see drawing near,
Turning from one way to another and then becoming universal,
So great and long, that they shall come to pluck,
The root from the wood and the child from the breast.

A great famine do I see drawing near, states that immediately following World War 3 there is no worldwide famine.

However, as the radiation poisoning from the war moves
from the atmosphere into the ground, fertile land becomes
sterile. Eventually, this sterile land becomes universal across
the globe, and new ways to manufacture food like large
greenhouses will become the norm. This will take years
to gear up for however, and before this can happen food
will be very scarce for many people. The Great Famine
will be longer than people realize at first. Prior to World
War 3, people will need to store up food and water,
in order to survive for a period
from two to five years.

Century I 68

O what a horrid and sad torment,
Shall be put to three innocents,
Poison shall be suspected, evil guards shall betray them,
They shall be put to horror by drunken executioners.

This tells us that President Putin of Russia, will be killed
by evil guards, and three innocent people will be charged.
Poison shall be suspected, evil guards shall betray them,
explains that poison shall be suspected.

Century I 69

The great mountain encompasses seven stadia,
After peace, war, famine, and inundation,
Shall tumble a great way, sinking great countries,
Even ancient houses and their great foundations.

The Chinese economy is described as a Great
Mountain, that will collapse before the end of the 21st Century.
Even ancient houses and their great foundations, implies
those countries, corporations, and individual that
are long established in China, will fail and sink.

Century I 70

Rain, famine, war in Persia having not ceased,
Too great credulity shall betray the Monarch,
Being ended there, it shall commence in France,
A secret omen to one that he shall die.

A terrorist leader of Iran, shall claim innocence,
after the first nuclear explosion in France. Iran will say
they have nothing to do with these nuclear attacks, even
though the explosive material points in their direction.

President Putin of Russia, who started the attacks on France
and Europe, will see the first nuclear explosion
as *a secret omen* that his death is near.

Great Quatrain 20

(Century I 79/Century I 80/Century I 81/Century I 82)

Interpretation:

World War 3
Nine Nuclear Nations

Summary:

Of the nine nuclear nations nearly, all will see 10%
of their population killed, 8% banished, and 11% scattered.
Bordeaux will be destroyed by a nuclear blast. Nuclear
explosions will be evident in March, April, May and June.
Vienna will see people leave the city, after a nuclear
explosion in a forest nearby.

Century I 79

Bazax, Lectore, Condon, Auch, Agine,
Being moved by laws, quarrels and monopoly,
They shall put to ruin Bordeaux, Toulouse, Bayonne,
Going about to renew their Tauropole.

Bazax, Lectore, Condon, Auch, Agine, being moved
by laws, quarrels and monopoly, are all cities that form
the edge of a blast site in Gascony. The new people coming
into France will bring their own laws and quarrels, and they
will have a monopoly on the situation. The state of France
will be in turmoil from the nuclear blasts, and will
be unable to focus on anything else.

They shall put to ruin Bordeaux, Toulouse, Bayonne,
going about to renew their Tauropole, states that Bordeaux,
and surrounding area, will suffer from a nuclear blast.
There will be more explosions from mini-subs
in the rivers still to come.

Century I 80

From the sixth bright celestial splendour,
Shall come very great lightning to Burgundy,
After which shall be born a monster of a hideous beast,
In March, April, May and June shall be great quarrelling
and muttering.

From the sixth bright celestial splendour, shall come very
great lightning to Burgundy. All Burgundy will be lit up,
from the explosions in France. *After which shall be born*
a monster of a hideous beast, in March, April, May and June
shall be great quarrelling and muttering, implies that after
Burgundy is lit up, the beast or hydrogen bomb, will
cause arguments among NATO leaders from
March until the end of June.

Century I 81

Of the human flock, nine shall be set aside,
Being divided in judgement and counsel,
Their destiny shall be to be divided,
Kappa, Theta, Lambda, dead, banished, scattered.

Of the human flock, nine shall be set aside, being divided in judgement and council, tells us that the world will set aside nine nations that have nuclear weapons, namely, the United States, Russia, United Kingdom, France, China, India, Pakistan, North Korea, and Israel. They will be divided at the United Nations, as well as in their judgement. *Their destiny will be to be divided, Kappa, Theta, Lambda, dead, banished, scattered*, states that these nine countries during World War 3, will have nearly 10% of their population killed, 8% banished, and 11% scattered.

Century I 82

When the wooden columns shall be shaken,
By the stern wind and covered by ruby hue,
Then shall go out a great assembly,
And Vienna and the land of Austria shall tremble.

When the wooden columns shall be shaken, by a stern wind and covered by a ruby hue, describes a nuclear explosion in a forest near Vienna. The destruction of the forest, as well as a wind and a red glow are revealed. *Then shall go out a great assembly, and Vienna and the land of Austria shall tremble*, states that the nuclear explosion near Vienna, will cause people to flee the city as the ground shakes.

51

Great Quatrain 21

(Century I 83/Century I 84/Century I 85/Century I 86)

Interpretation:

World War 3
Woman Chinese Premiere

Summary:

The Woman Chinese Premiere will make statements that are inconsistent with President Putin of Russia, even though they have a Joint Military Structure. The Exiles and Barbarians coming into Southern France from Spain, will begin to divide up the land and estates among themselves. At this time, the earth's atmosphere changes, causing the moon to be obscured. A new United States Military leader will be sworn in. President Putin will have two clones made of himself, and both will die in World War 3.

Century I 83

The alien agent shall divide booties,
Saturn and Mars shall have his aspect furious,
Horrid and strange to the Tuscans and Latin's,
The Grecians shall be curious to strike.

The alien agent shall divide the booties, tells us that the Exile people invading France from Spain, will divide the land and estates among themselves.

This will cause a furious response from the French population. *Horrid and strange to the Tuscans, the Grecians shall be curious to strike* infers that in Italy, people will view the Exiles and Barbarians with horror, as they commit many crimes. The Greeks will be slow to react, out of curiosity.

Century I 84

The moon shall be obscured in the deepest darkness,
Her brother shall pass being of a ferruginous colour,
The great one long hidden under shadows,
Shall make his iron lukewarm in the bloody rain.

The moon shall be obscured in the deepest darkness, her brother shall pass being of a ferruginous colour, implies that the nuclear explosions will start to change the world's atmosphere, such that the moon will not be seen at night, and the sun will have a red tinge to it. *The great one long hidden under shadows, shall make his iron lukewarm in the bloody rain* states that there will be a new U.S. Military leader in the Pentagon, when the atmosphere changes.

Century I 85

A king shall be troubled by the answer of a lady,
Ambassadors shall despise their lives,
The great one being undecided, shall counterfeit his brothers,
They shall die by two, anger, hatred, and envy.

A king shall be troubled by the answer of a lady, ambassadors will despise their lives, tells us that the Woman Premiere of China, is making statements that are inconsistent with President Putin of Russia, even though they have combined their armed forces. Ambassadors between these countries, will need to find a common ground. *The great one being undecided shall counterfeit his brothers, they shall die by two, anger, hatred and envy,* suggests that President Putin of Russia will have two clones of himself made, that will eventually die together during World War 3.

Century I 86

When the queen shall see herself vanquished,
She shall do a masculine courage,
Upon a horse, she shall pass over the river naked,
Followed by iron she shall do wrong to her faith.

When the queen shall see herself vanquished, she shall do a deed of masculine courage, states that the Woman Premiere of China will do a courageous act, even though she has lost the war. *Upon a horse she shall pass over the river naked, followed by iron she shall do wrong to her faith.* This predicts that the Woman Premiere of China will cross a river by boat, and take over the north eastern part of Russia. She will be followed by her army, and say that this is by previous agreement with President Putin. However, most people in China don't think this should have been done, and they are highly critical of her and this move.

54

Great Quatrain 38

(Century II 49/Century II 50/Century II 51/Century II 52)

Interpretation:

World War 3
Two Great Wrestlers

Summary:

World War 3 will be caused by two great wrestlers, namely President Putin of Russia and the Woman Premiere of China. Both are Judo experts in wrestling. There will be a siege of NATO Forces in northern Belgium. Missiles from Russian nuclear submarines will rain down on England, in three waves of 26. The Queen will pass away. The North Pole will be destroyed, and sea levels will rise immediately.

Century II 49

The councillors of the first monopoly,
The conqueror being seduced by the Melite,
Rhodes, Bizance, for exposing their pole,
The ground shall fail the followers of the runways.

The councillors of the first monopoly, or Russia and China, are *exposed* in their plans. The United States aircraft carrier, or *the followers of runways,* will control *the ground* as well as the air.

Century II 50

When those of Hainault, of Gand and Brussels,
Shall see the siege laid before Langres,
Behind their sides shall be cruel wars,
The old wound shall be worse than enemies.

Hainault, and *Gand or Ghent* in Northern Belgium, where NATO's HQ is based, will see *Langres in siege* from the Russian and Barbarian troops. There will be *cruel wars* behind the siege lines. However, this will be nothing, compared with the nuclear explosions in France.

Century II 51

The blood of the just shall dry in London,
Burnt by fire of three times twenty-six,
The ancient dame shall fall from her high place,
Of the same sect many shall be killed.

Missiles will come from Russian submarines, by three waves of 26, targeting England. This will cause deaths and injury in *London*. The Queen of England will pass away, and many of her aristocracy will be killed or injured.

Century II 52

During many nights the earth shall quake,
About the spring, two great earthquakes shall follow one another,
Corinth, Ephesus shall swim in the twin seas,
War shall be moved by two great wrestlers.

World War 3 is caused by *two great wrestlers*. They are
President Putin of Russia and the Woman Premiere of China,
who are both Judo wrestlers. In spring, close to April and May,
there will be war with the exchange of nuclear weapons,
such that *the earth will quake*. When the North Pole
is destroyed, there is a rise in sea levels immediately
afterwards. This results in the death of millions
or possibly billions, by floods, environmental
changes, and radically different coastlines
around the world.

Great Quatrain 39

(Century II 53/Century II 54/Century II 55/Century II 56)

Interpretation:

World War 3
The Crown

Summary:

The British Navy will not cease, until they are revenged on the Russian fleets for the deaths caused in London. New York is troubled because of their proximity to the rivers, and potentially a Russian mini-sub.

Century II 53

The great plague of the maritime city,
Shall not cease until the death be revenged,
Of the just blood by price condemned without crime,
Of the great dame not feigned abused.

London, *the maritime city*, is hit with radiation poisoning. The British will not cease until all the deaths incurred by the Russian fleet are *revenged.*

Century II 54

By a strange people and a remote nation,
The great city near the water shall be much troubled,
The girl without great difference for an estate,
The chief frightened, at not having been warned.

New York *will be troubled* by Russia and China, the *remote nations*. They are concerned about their proximity to the rivers, and a potential Russian mini-sub.

Century II 55

In the fight the great one, who was but little worth,
At his last endeavour shall do a wonderful thing,
While Adria shall see what was wanting,
In the banquet he shall stab the proud one.

A leader in northern Italy, shall do a courageous act, and assassinate the Barbarian leader at a *banquet.*

Century II 56

He whom neither plague nor sword could destroy,
Shall die in the rain being stricken by thunder,
The abbot shall die when he shall see ruined,
Those in the shipwreck, striving to catch hold of the rock.

The Abbot, in Italy will witness a *shipwreck* far inland, after the nuclear explosion. He shall see Russian sailors striving *to catch a rock. The Abbot* will die from radiation exposure.

Great Quatrain 40

(Century II 57/Century II 58/Century II 59/Century II 60)

Interpretation:

World War 3
American Aircraft Carrier Sunk

Summary:

An American Aircraft Carrier and five ships, will be sunk from a nuclear explosion caused by a mini-sub. A Mini-sub manned by a terrorist, will make its way into the harbour of Marseille. Israel will be struck with a nuclear weapon, as well as the Rhone, Loire, and Tagus Rivers. Russia, China, and Iran, will break their international agreements, causing the West to go on a war footing.

Century II 57

Before the battle, the great wall shall fall,
The great one to death, too sudden and bewailed,
The boat being imperfect the most part shall swim,
Near the river the earth shall be dyed with blood.

The wall shall fall, tells us that the American NATO Fleet, in the Mediterranean, will be attacked by a Russian mini-sub. *The great one, will die suddenly,* implying the American Admiral will die. Sailors will try *swimming* for shore.

Century II 58

Without foot or hand, sharp and strong teeth,
By a globe, in the middle of the port, and the first born,
Near the gate shall be transported by a traitor,
The moon shineth, the little great one carried away.

A Mini-sub with a terrorist, will find its way into
the middle of the Port of Marseille. He will be aided
by *a traitor*, who will open the gate. The terrorist
in the mini-sub, is the older brother of the two,
or *the first born*. The nuclear warhead will be of a strange
design, perfectly round. The leader of Marseille
will die in the explosion, which will occur
at night while *the moon shines.*

Century II 59

The French Fleet by the help of the great guards,
Of great Neptune, and his trident soldiers,
Shall gnaw Provence by keeping great company,
Also, Mars shall plague Narbonne by javelots and darts.

The French Fleet will be helped by the American Fleet.
They shall put Marines in *Provence*, north of Nice.
Narbonne will be attacked by the
Exiles from Spain.

Century II 60

The Punic Faith broken in the east,
Great Jud, and Rhone, Loire and Tagus shall be changed,
When the mule's hunger shall be satisfied,
The fleet scattered, blood and bodies shall swim.

The countries of *the East*, Russia and China, will break their international agreements. Great Israel will be attacked with missiles, and one will hit. The Rhone, Loire, and the Tagus rivers, will all experience nuclear explosions from mini-subs, which will *change* their flow. Food will be scarce in Europe. The NATO *Fleet* in the Mediterranean, will be *scattered* for safety.

Great Quatrain 43

(Century II 69/Century II 70/Century II 71/Century II 72)

Interpretation:

World War 3
Darts from Heaven

Summary:

Missiles, or darts from heaven, are exchanged over the North Pole. Some people will die speaking. Russia and China will lose all their nuclear weapons, and look for atonement. An Exile leader will take over most of France. The Exile leader of Sicily will bring food, in exchange for power.

Century II 69

The French King, by the Celtic right hand,
Seeing the discord of the great Monarchy,
Upon three parts of it, will make his sceptre to flourish,
Against the cap of the great Hierarchy.

A French King or Exile leader, will see the *discord of the monarchy* or French government. He will set up his own government, which will control *three parts* or ¾'s of France. *Against the cap of the great hierarchy,* tells us that he is against NATO and the United States.

Century II 70

The dart of heaven shall make his circuit,
Some die speaking, a great execution,
The stone in the tree, the fierce people humbled,
Human noise, a monster purged by expiation.

The dart of heaven, or missiles from above, will hit some populated areas, causing people to *die while speaking*. The *fierce people* from Russia, *will be humbled* after their defeat.

Century II 71

The banished person shall come into Sicily,
To free the foreign nation from hunger,
In the dawning of the day the Celts shall fail them,
Their life shall be preserved, the King shall submit
to reason.

The banished person or Exile leader from Russia, will come back to Sicily with food, in exchange for power.

Century II 72

The French Army shall be vexed in Italy,
On all sides fighting, and a great loss,
The Romans run away, and though France, repulsed,
Near the Ticino, by Rubicon the fight shall be doubtful.

The French Army in Provence, with American Forces, will fight the incoming Barbarians from Russia, *near Ticino and the Rubicon*. French Forces will repulse the Barbarians.

Great Quatrain 46

(Century II 81/Century II 82/Century II 83/Century II 84)

Interpretation:

World War 3
The Great Flood

Summary:

The Great Flood will be caused by the destruction
of the North Pole, which will lead to a rise in sea levels.
Missiles will cause the city of Moscow to be mostly burnt.
Russia will experience hunger and starvation,
caused by the Exiles and Barbarians that
strip the country of food.

Century II 81

By fire from Heaven the city shall be almost burnt,
The waters threaten another Deucalion,
Sardinia shall be vexed by the African fleet,
After that Libra shall have left her Phaeton.

By fire from heaven, implying from incoming missiles, *the city* Moscow is *almost* entirely *burnt*. The vaporization of the North Pole, will cause an immediate rise in sea levels, *threatening another Deucalion*, or worldwide flood. Sardinia shall be inundated by Barbarians from the *African Fleet*.

Century II 82

By hunger, the prey shall make the wolf prisoner,
Assaulting him then in great distress,
The eldest having got before the last,
The great one does not escape in the middle of the crowd.

By hunger, the United States will *make the wolf prisoner*, suggests that Russia will face starvation. Russia has been stripped of food by both the Exile boat people, as well as by the Barbarians. President Putin of Russia, hiding in Europe under a disguise, is recognized *in the middle of the crowd.* He is captured, and later dies in bed from evil guards.

Century II 83

The great trade of the great Lion altered,
The most part turns into pristine ruin,
Shall become a prey to soldiers and reaped by wound,
In Mount Jura and Suabia great fogs.

World War 3 will cause a change *in the great trade,* or trading pattern of Britain and the continent. While the Barbarians move through Europe, Britain's trade with the continent will cease. In Germany and in Hungary, there will *be great fogs* or confusion, with no clear indication as to events. The Barbarians will prey on the citizens of Europe, especially after they are wounded, or *reaped by wound.*

Century II 84

Between Campania, Sienna, Pisa and Ostia,
For six months and nine days there shall be no rain,
The strange language in Dalmatian land,
Shall overrun, spoiling all the country.

In northern Italy, after the nuclear explosion, *there is no rain for six months. The strange language* heard is Ragusa, an ancient language of Dalmatia. This language is now heard and spoken, after *Dalmatia* declares independence. However, they too are invaded by Barbarians and *overrun, spoiling all the country.*

Great Quatrain 49

(Century II 93/Century II 94/Century II 95/Century II 96)

Interpretation:

World War 3
Cities Deserted

Summary:

Throughout the world, all the cities are deserted as people seek the safety of their own Ark. At the entrance to the Tiber River, there will be a nuclear explosion before the destruction of the North Pole. Of the million Barbarians that enter Europe, less than a quarter of one million will survive. They shall divide up the fields in Europe among themselves,
even though they know nothing about agriculture.

Century II 93

Near the Tiber, going towards Libra,
A little before the great inundation,
The master of the ship being taken, shall be put into a well,
And a castle and a palace shall be burnt.

A captain from Russia, will be held captive in a prison.
Those that are hiding in a *castle and a palace*,
shall be burnt when it is hit by fire.

Century II 94

Great Po shall receive great harm from the French,
A vain terror shall seize upon the maritime lion,
Infinite people shall go beyond the sea,
Which shall not escape even a quarter of a million.

The great Po shall be changed when French troops from Provence, come into Italy to stop the advancing Barbarians. At this time, England is in fear of Russian nuclear submarines off its coast. Of the 1 million Barbarians, less than *a quarter of one million* will survive.

Century II 95

The populous places shall be deserted,
A great division to obtain fields,
Kingdom given to prudent incapable,
When the great brothers shall die by dissension.

Throughout the world, all *the populous places shall be deserted,* as people seek safety in their own Arks. The Barbarians will divide up the fields among themselves, even though they know nothing about agriculture. Two *great brothers,* who are terrorists, *shall die by dissension,* or by exploding their mini-subs.

Century II 96

A burning shall be seen by night in Heaven,
Near the end and the beginning of the Rhone,
Famine, sword, too late help shall be provided,
Persia shall come against Macedonia.

People looking toward Marseille, *near the end*
of the Rhone, will see a great *burning* in the sky
from the first explosion. While those who look toward
the *beginning of the Rhone*, will see another nuclear
explosion at Chartres. Also, Barbarians from Iran
will be coming through Turkey, and into Greece
from the Middle East.

Great Quatrain 54

(Century III 13/Century III 14/Century III 15/Century III 16)

Interpretation:

World War 3
The Ark

Summary:

Some people that are hiding in their Ark in World War 3, will be killed because of their proximity to the blasts. China will takeover the eastern portion of Russia, at the end of World War 3. King Charles will have two assassination attempts on his life, and will survive both and prosper. During World War 3 many French children will suffer, due to the changing environmental conditions, radiation poisoning, and famine.

Century III 13

In the ark, lightning, gold and silver melted,
Of two prisoners, one shall eat up the other,
The greatest of the city shall be laid down,
When the navy that was drowned shall swim.

In World War 3, people across the world will be *in the ark* hiding for their own personal safety. Some people will still be killed in their Ark, because of their proximity to the nuclear explosions.

Of two prisoners, one shall eat up the other, states that after
Russia and China are defeated, China will move into eastern
Russia and claim it by previous agreement. *The greatest of the city
shall be laid down* is Moscow, which is defeated and laid low
by American Armed Forces. *When the navy that was drowned
shall swim,* suggests that the Americans will come back
from their defeat at the start of the war, to win.

Century III 14

By the branch of the valiant personage,
Of weak France, by the unfortunate father,
Honours, riches, labour in his old age,
For having believed the counsel of a nice man.

By the branch of the valiant personage, the leader with
Royal blood, namely King Charles, will receive *honours,
riches,* and *labour in his old age.* During World War 3
when France is weak, he will take the *counsel
of a nice man* or a good person,
and win renown.

Century III 15

Heart, vigour and glory shall change the Kingdom,
In all points, having an adversary against it,
Then shall France overcome childhood by death,
The greatest Regent shall then be most contrary to it.

Despite having a fierce adversary in World War 3,
France does not give up and continues to fight
with *heart, vigour and glory.*

The reality however, is that many French children are
killed as a result of the war, from radiation and famine.
This puts into question the very survival of the French state.
At that time, the Barbarian leader of France, *the greatest regent*
will be most against the French state, and its survival.

Century III 16

The English Prince Mars has his heart from Heaven,
Will follow his prosperous fortune,
Of two duels, one shall pierce the gall,
Being hated of him, and beloved of his mother.

During World War 3, *the English Prince Mars* at war
is Prince Charles, who becomes King Charles. He *will follow*
his prosperous fortune, and become King of the United Kingdom.
However, there will be two assassination attempts on his life,
such that *one shall pierce the gall,* or the gall bladder.
Although the soldier that did this deed is hated
by everyone, he is *beloved of his mother.*

Great Quatrain 60

(Century III 37/Century III 38/Century III 39/Century III 40)

Interpretation:

World War 3
The United States and
NATO Win Air War

Summary:

The United States and NATO will win the Air War,
in World War 3. People will start to follow the Air War,
as a great theatre. American and NATO Forces will
say a prayer, before beginning operations. They shall
cause the ancient wall of China to be destroyed,
inferring that they will remove China as a threat.

Century III 37

Before the assault, the prayer shall be said,
A kite shall be taken by the eagle, being deceived by an ambuscade,
The ancient wall shall be beaten down with cannons,
By fire and blood, a few shall have quarter.

Before the assault on the east during World War 3,
the United States Military will say a prayer. American
Air power will cause *the ancient wall* of China
to be destroyed, inferring that China
will be removed as a threat.

Century III 38

The French people and another nation,
Being over the mountains, shall die and be taken,
In a month contrary to them, and near the vintage,
By the Lords agreed together.

The French people and the Italian people, going mostly to the Alps for protection from the nuclear explosions, will be forced in the month of May or *near the vintage*, to return home. This will be a month *contrary to them* and France.

Century III 39

The seven shall agree together within three months,
To conquer the Apennine Alps,
But the tempest and the cowardly Genoese,
Shall sink them into sudden ruin.

The seven leaders of the West will agree to send troops to fight the Barbarians, that are still hiding in the Italian mountains. These Barbarians are making raids, on the cities in the region. However, the Barbarians will get word of this from *the cowardly Genoese*.

Century III 40

The great Theatre shall be raised up again,
The die being cast and the net spread,
The first too much in tolling shall weary,
Beaten down by bows, who long before were split.

The great theatre of the sky, or battles in the sky,
will be *raised up again* by people following the war.
The Russian Air Force will gradually lose, to the American
NATO Forces. *The die being cast,* implies that this was
a forgone conclusion, to some extent. *Beaten down
by bows, who long before were split,* suggests that
American Naval power is winning the Air War,
coming back from a defeat at the
start of the war.

Great Quatrain 64

(Century III 53/Century III 54/Century III 55/Century III 56)

Interpretation:

World War 3
607 Missiles in Three Waves

Summary:

There will be 607 missiles in three waves, sent over the North Pole by Russia, targeting the United States and Canada. A leader of the Barbarians will take over Nuremberg, Augsburg, and capture Frankfort. One of the Barbarians will leave Paris, and go to southern Spain, destroying everything in his path. At the end of March, the nuclear explosion at Rouen Bridge will occur. Montpellier will be destroyed also.

Century III 53

When the great one shall carry the prize,
Of Nuremberg, Augsburg and Basel,
By Agrippina the Chief of Frankfort shall be taken,
They shall go through Flanders as far as France.

When the great one shall carry the prize, then President Putin of Russia, traveling in disguise, shall take control of Nuremberg and Augsburg.

Then an older German woman shall help him find
and capture, the *chief of Frankfort*. Russian troops,
along with Barbarians will then head *through Flanders*,
where they will be stopped by British troops.

Century III 54

One of the greatest shall run away into Spain,
That shall cause a wound to bleed long,
Leading armies over high mountains,
Destroying all, and afterwards shall reign.

One of the greatest shall run away into Spain,
states that one of the Barbarian leaders will leave Paris,
and go into Spain, *destroying all* or everything in his way.
He will then *reign* in Spain. This will cause the *wound*
of the war, to stay longer than expected. Although
he will take control of Grenada, he will
afterwards be arrested for war crimes.

Century III 55

In the year that one eye shall reign in France,
The court shall be in the very same trouble,
The great one of Blois shall kill his friend,
The kingdom shall be in an evil way, and double doubt.

One of the Barbarian leaders *shall reign in France.*
He has only one eye. In the year that he takes control
of France, or what is left of France, his court
will be in trouble from internal dissension.

The *great one of Blois shall kill his friend,*
and people will be in doubt, as to whether the Exiles
can control anything.

Century III 56

Montauban, Nismes, Avignon and Besier,
Plague, lightning and hail at the end of March,
The Bridge of Paris, the Wall of Lyons,
and Montpellier shall fall,
From six hundred and seven score three parts.

The people of *Montauban, Nismes, Avignon and Besier,* are towns just outside the nuclear blast site near Marseille. They will face disease, radiation poisoning, and deadly *hail at the end of March*. The *Bridge of Paris*, is the Rouen Bridge, where the explosion closest to Paris will occur. The *wall of Lyon* is the crest wall, from a nuclear explosion near Marseille. Montpellier will be completely gone. Shortly afterwards in May, the Russians will launch a missile attack on the United States and Canada, with *six hundred and seven* missiles, over the North Pole in three waves.

Great Quatrain 78

(Century IV 9/Century IV 10/Century IV 11/Century IV 12)

Interpretation:

World War 3
The 12 Red Ones

Summary:

President Putin of Russia, will be induced
to commit a great act. He will provide the twelve
red ones, or terrorists, with nuclear weapons and
mini-subs to destroy the ports of Europe. The Russian
President will be wounded in both thighs, in the middle
of a crowd of Exiles. He will be in disguise, as he travels
through Europe with the Barbarians. The Exiles and
Barbarians will have their camp routed by NATO,
and finally, be driven out of France completely.

Century IV 9

The chief of the camp in the middle of the crowd,
Shall be wounded with an arrow through both his thighs,
When Geneva being in tears and distress,
Shall be betrayed by Lausanne and the Swiss.

President Putin of Russia, being *in the middle*
of a crowd of Exiles, will be *wounded* in *both thighs*.
Geneva will be in *distress* over President Putin,
and as a result, *they shall be betrayed*
or exposed in their loyalties.

Century IV 10

The young prince being falsely accused,
Shall put the camp in trouble and in quarrels,
The chief shall be murdered by the tumult,
The sceptre shall be appeased and later cure
the king's evil.

A young prince or young leader of the Exile group, will be *falsely accused*, and as a result there will be *trouble and quarrels* in the Exile camp. *The chief shall be murdered by the tumult,* tells us that the older leader of the Exiles *shall be murdered* in the confusion. The West shall be somewhat *appeased* by this outcome.

Century IV 11

He that shall be covered with a great cloak,
Shall be induced to commit some great act,
The twelve red ones shall soil the table cloth,
Under murder, murder shall be committed.

The one *covered with a great cloak*, is President Putin of Russia in disguise, moving with the Barbarians in Europe. He shall be the one who causes the *twelve red ones* or twelve terrorists, *to commit some great act*. The *great act* that Nostradamus is referring to, is the act of exploding nuclear weapons in the ports and rivers of Europe, using Russian mini-subs with Russian training.

Century IV 12

The greatest camp being in disorder shall be routed,
And shall be pursued not much after,
The army shall encamp again, and the troops set in order,
Then afterwards, they shall be wholly
driven out of France.

The greatest camp being in disorder shall be routed, explains that the great camp of the Exiles and Barbarians, will eventually be routed by NATO Forces. *The army shall encamp again, and the troops set in order,* infers that they will re-establish their camp, and set their troops in order. However, after that they will be completely *driven out of France* by NATO.

Great Quatrain 88

(Century IV 49/Century IV 50/Century IV 51/Century IV 52)

Interpretation:

World War 3
The Guillotine Returns

Summary:

When the Barbarians takeover Paris, the Guillotine returns, with public executions similar to the Reign of Terror during the French Revolution. Justice will finally be served in Spain, after the Barbarians leave. Chinese forces will perish without a witness, but not before the seven nuclear explosions occur suddenly from Mini-subs in Europe. China will attack India, and lose the battle near the Ganges River.

Century IV 49

Before the people, blood shall be spilt,
Who shall not come far from high heaven,
But it shall not be heard of for a great while,
The spirit of one shall come to witness it.

In Paris, the new government from the Barbarians
with an Arab leader, will bring back the guillotine,
which *shall not be heard of for a great while.*
There will be public executions once again,
before the people as in the French
Revolution.

Those that are believed to be against the Barbarian cause, will go to the guillotine, recalling *the spirit* of Robespierre and the Reign of Terror.

Century IV 50

Libra shall see Spain to reign,
And have the monarchy of Heaven and Earth,
Nobody shall see the forces of Asia to perish,
Till seven have kept the Hierarchy successively.

Libra shall see Spain to reign, informs us that justice will eventually be seen in Spain, after the Barbarians are forced to leave and a new government is brought in. *Nobody shall see the forces of Asia to perish,* tells us that when the forces of China perish, no one will witness this event. However, this will not occur, until the seven nuclear explosions by the terrorists with Russian mini-subs are complete.

Century IV 51

A Duke being in the pursuit of his enemy,
Shall come in, hindering the falange,
Hastened on foot shall follow them so close,
That the day of battle shall be near Ganges.

Indian Forces under a Duke, shall be *in the pursuit* of the Chinese military on foot, as they flee northern India. The *battle shall be near Ganges,* or the Ganges River. In the battle between India and China, China will lose.

Century IV 52

In a besieged city, men and women being upon the walls,
The enemy without, the governor ready to surrender,
The wind shall be strong against the soldiers,
They shall be driven away by lime dust and cinders.

In a besieged city, men and women being upon the walls, suggests that citizens in a castle in southern France, will be surrounded by Exiles and Barbarians. Both men and women will man the walls. The governor of the city will be *ready to surrender.* However, the enemy is finally *driven away,* with fire and explosions from NATO planes.

Great Quatrain 94

(Century IV 73/Century IV 74/Century IV 75/Century IV 76)

Interpretation:

World War 3
The White Country

Summary:

The United States and Russia will battle over the
North Pole in the white country, and the United States
will win. The great nephew, a high-ranking U.S. Military
officer, will provoke a Barbarian leader to a cowardly act.
This Barbarian will have a mock trial in the evening,
and execute the President of Italy. The Exiles
and Barbarians will set up their own
United Nations at Geneva.

Century IV 73

The great nephew by force shall provoke,
The sin committed by a pusillanimous heart,
Ferrari and Asti shall make a trial of the Duke,
When the pantomime shall be in the evening.

The great nephew, a U.S. Military officer, will
provoke a cowardly heart among the Barbarians to commit
a sin. There will be *a trial* of an innocent Italian leader,
and a relative of *Ferrari, and Asti, shall make* the *trial*.
This will be a *pantomime* or mock trial
in the evening, followed
by his execution.

Century IV 74

From Lake Geneva and to Verona,
They shall be gathered against those of England,
Great many Germans and many more mercenaries,
Shall be routed together with many people.

They shall be gathered against those of England, implies there will be a gathering of the Exiles and Barbarians from *Geneva and to Verona* against the West. This will be orchestrated by Russia. *Great many Germans and many more mercenaries,* shall set up their own United Nations in *Geneva*. Eventually they shall all *be routed together with many people,* at the end of World War 3, and forced to surrender
or leave Europe.

Century IV 75

One being ready to fight shall faint,
The chief of the adverse party shall obtain the victory,
The rear guard shall fight it out,
Those that fall away shall die in the white country.

There will be a battle over the North Pole between Russia and the United States, *in the white country. Those that fall away* from high altitude warfare, will *die* in the bitter cold of the Arctic and Canada. *The chief of the adverse party shall obtain the victory,* informs us that the United States will win the battle over the North Pole, and the Russian *rear guard* will have
to fight it out.

Century IV 76

The Nictobriges by those of Perigort,
Shall be vexed as far as the Rhone,
The associate of the Gascons and Bigorre,
Shall betray the church while the priest is in the pulpit.

Those of Agen, *by those of Perigort,* will *be vexed* or worried after *the Rhone* River is destroyed in the Marseille nuclear blast. An *associate,* who is a terrorist, will *betray the* Mosque *while the priest is still in the pulpit.*

Great Quatrain 103

(Century V 9/Century V 10/Century V 11/Century V 12)

Interpretation:

World War 3
Solar Ship

Summary:

The Woman Premiere of China, will make her way back from Europe, in a ship that has solar energy. She will announce that China, is no longer part of the Russian military joint command structure. When she arrives at Hong Kong, she will be arrested, and thrust out of power.

Century V 9

At the bottom of the great evil arch,
By a chief that is captive, the friend shall be anticipated,
One shall be born of a lady, with hairy face and forehead,
Then by craft shall a Duke be put to death.

The *chief that is captive* by his *arch* enemy, will *anticipate* help, from *one born* from a *hairy* woman. However, by a trick, the *Duke* shall *be put to death*.

Century V 10

A Celtic leader wounded in battle,
Near a cellar, seeing death about to overthrow his people,
Being much oppressed with blood, wounds and enemies,
Is succoured by four unknowns.

A *leader* of the Barbarians will be wounded
and near *death*, when *four unknown* people help
him, near a wine *cellar*.

Century V 11

Sea by solars, she shall pass safely,
Those of Venus shall hold all of Africa,
Saturn shall hold their kingdom no longer,
And shall change the Asiatic port.

The Woman Premiere of China, will make her way back
from Europe, in a ship that has *solar* energy. The United
States will control *all of Africa*. She shall announce that
China, is *no longer* part of the Russian military. When she
arrives at *the Asiatic port* or Hong Kong, she is arrested.

Century V 12

Near Lake Geneva shall be a plot,
By a strange whore to betray a city,
Before she be killed, her great retinue will come to Augsburg,
And those of the Rhine shall come to invade her.

Near Lake Geneva, a lady will *betray the city,* and make
for *Augsburg. She will be killed* along with *her retinue.*

Great Quatrain 110

(Century V 37/Century V 38/Century V 39/Century V 40)

Interpretation:

World War 3
The Three Hundred

Summary:

Three hundred of the Barbarian leaders, will be of one mind, to succeed in taking over Europe in twenty months. The twenty months, that are given to President Putin of Russia and the Barbarian leaders, are from the beginning of 2024 until August 2025.

Century V 37

Three hundred shall be of one mind and agreement,
That they may attain their ends,
Twenty months after by all of them and their partners
Their King shall be betrayed by simulating a feigned hatred.

Three hundred of the Barbarian leaders will be *of one mind*, to succeed in taking over Europe in *twenty months* or less. The twenty months, that are given to President Putin of Russia and the Barbarian leaders, are from the beginning of 2024 until August 2025.

Century V 38

The great monarch that shall succeed to the great one,
Shall lead a life unlawful and lecherous,
By carelessness he shall give to all,
So that in conclusion, the Salic law will fail.

A Barbarian leader in Germany, *will succeed to the*
great one, the President of Russia. He won't be able
to enforce normal civil laws, hence leading to anarchy.

Century V 39

Issued out of the true branch of the city,
He shall be set for heir of Etruria,
His ancient blood weaned by a long while,
Shall cause Florence to flourish in the coat of arms.

An Italian politician, who joins the Barbarians, will claim
part of northern Italy and Florence for himself.

Century V 40

The Royal blood shall be so much mixed,
The French shall be constrained by the Spaniards,
They shall stay till the term is past,
And the remembrance of the voice is over.

The Royal blood in France, is *so mixed*, that the French
will see their Barbarian leader as mainly *Spanish*, not French.
NATO will *stay* afterwards, until the remembrance
of his voice is gone.

Great Quatrain 116

(Century V 61/Century V 62/Century V 63/Century V 64)

Interpretation:

World War 3
Trident Taken

Summary:

The United States Navy will take the trident, inferring
that they will take control of all the oceans and seas of the
world. They will destroy all Russian and Chinese fleets, ships,
and submarines during World War 3. NATO ships
in the Mediterranean Sea, will be scattered for reasons
of safety. A radiation cloud near Bordeaux, will kill people
as it moves. Communities all through France, will be
asking for assistance.

Century V 61

The child of the great one that was not at his birth,
Shall subdue the high Apennine Mountains,
Shall make all those under Libra to quake,
From Mount Feurs, as far as Mount Cenis.

A *child* of illegitimate *birth*, will *subdue* northern Italy
for the Russians, and make all those who love freedom
concerned. From northern Rhone to Genoa, people will
quake in fear.

\

Century V 62

It shall rain blood upon the rocks,
The sun being in the east, and Saturn in the West,
War shall be near Orgon and a great evil at Rome,
Ships shall be cast away, and the trident be taken.

Blood shall be spilt *upon the rocks* in both Japan and the United States. *War will be near Orgon*, or Oregon, and *at Rome*, when the United States takes *the trident*.

Century V 63

Honour brings a complaint against a vain undertaking,
Galleys shall wander through the Latin seas, cold, hunger,
Not far from Tiber, the earth shall be dyed with blood,
And upon mankind shall be various plagues.

There will be many ships in the Mediterranean, keeping a safe distance from one another. There is a nuclear explosion at the mouth of the Tiber River.

Century V 64

The assembly by the rest of the great number,
By land and sea shall recall their council,
Near Automne, Gennes, Cloud of the shadow,
In fields and towns, the chiefs shall be one against another.

All ambassadors throughout the world will be *recalled*.
At Bordeaux, there will be a radiation *cloud* killing people.

Great Quatrain 120

(Century V 77/Century V 78/Century V 79/Century V 80)

Interpretation:

World War 3
The Great Ogmion

Summary:

The great Ogmion, or Pentagon leader, will go to Istanbul, and expel the Barbarians there. He will establish good laws, and overturn bad laws. He will raise those who are humble, and he will worry Russia and China. He is unique.

Century V 77

All the degrees of Ecclesiastical honour,
Shall be changed into a Quirinal Dial,
Into Martial Quirinal, Flaminus,
After that, a King of France shall make it Vulcanal.

With war and flames from the nuclear explosions, the god of fire or *Vulcanal,* will cause destruction throughout *France.*

Century V 78

The two united shall not hold long,
Within thirteen years to the Barbarian Satrap,
They shall cause such loss on both sides,
That one shall bless the boat and its covering.

The two united shall not hold long, are the Russian
and Chinese military, and their joint command. The
Barbarians who come into Europe to run the Celtic countries,
will *cause such loss,* that one will *bless* the United States
Navy and it's ships and planes.

Century V 79

The sacred pomp shall bow down her wings,
At the coming of the great law giver,
He shall raise the humble and vex the rebellious,
No emulator of his shall be born.

The great Ogmion, or Pentagon Military leader, will
enter Europe as *the great law giver.* He will raise the humble,
and worry Russia and China. *No emulator of his shall be born.*
He is unique.

Century V 80

The Ogmion shall come near great Constantinople,
And shall expel the Barbarian League,
Of the two laws, the wicked one shall yield,
The Barbarian, and the French shall be in perpetual friction.

The great Ogmion will go to Istanbul, and *expel the*
Barbarians there. He will establish good laws and overturn
bad laws. The French who are with him, will be in perpetual
friction with *the Barbarians,* until they are destroyed.

Great Quatrain 121

(Century V 81/Century V 82/Century V 83/Century V 84)

Interpretation:

World War 3
The Eastern Wall Falls

Summary:

World War 3 will last seven months, from January 1st until the end of July, 2025. The eastern wall shall fall, tells us that Russia and China will fail against the United States. When defeat looks to be a real possibility to Russia and China, they will launch missiles at the United States over seven days. President Putin of Russia, who instigated the war, will not be seen. During the period of nuclear missile exchanges, the President of the United States will read a Bible at the table.

Century V 81

The Royal Bird upon the city of the Sun,
Seven months together shall make a nocturnal augury,
The Eastern wall shall fall, the lightning shall shine,
Then the enemies shall be at the gate for seven days.

The United States, or *Royal Bird,* will be set against the Russian vision of utopia, which Russia tries to sell as it moves through Europe.

Seven months together shall make a nocturnal augury,
states that from January until the end of July there will
be open war. *The enemies shall be at the gate for seven days.*
When defeat looks to be a real possibility to Russia and China,
they will launch missiles at the United States over seven days.
The eastern wall shall fall, implies Russia and China
are defeated at the end of July.

Century V 82

On the conclusion of the pact made, out of the fortress,
Shall not come he that was in despair,
When those of Arbois, of Langres, against Brescia,
Shall put in Dolle an ambuscade of foes.

On the conclusion of the pact made, to lay down arms,
President Putin of Russia will not be seen. However, there
will be put in place *an ambuscade of foes* at Dolle, of those
responsible for the nuclear blast at Brescia.

Century V 83

Those that shall have undertaken to subvert,
The kingdom that has no equal in power and victories,
Shall cause fraud, notice to be given for three nights together
When the greatest shall be reading a Bible at the table.

Those that shall have undertaken to subvert, the kingdom
that has no equal in power and victories, are the Russians
and Chinese, who are attacking the United States. When that
happens the President, leaving everything to his military,
will read a *Bible at the table.*

Century V 84

One shall be born out of the gulf and immeasurable city,
Born of parent's obscure and dark,
Who, by means of Rouen and Eureux,
Will go about to destroy the power of the great King.

One shall be born out of the gulf in Iran, who will be a terrorist and dictator. He will be responsible for the nuclear explosion at *Rouen*. He will *destroy the power of the great King,* suggesting he will be responsible for the killing of the President of France, and his advisors.

Great Quatrain 128

(Century VI 9/Century VI 10/Century VI 11/Century VI 12)

Interpretation:

World War 3
The Temple of Colours

Summary:

The temple of colours, is the Pentagon. The holy temples or Arks, are where people are hiding during World War 3. The Exiles and Barbarians will attack people that are hiding during the war, and they will even issue medals of gold and silver to commemorate this bad behaviour. The nine nuclear nations will be reduced to seven, after Russia and China lose their nuclear arsenals. This will then be followed by a further reduction, from seven nuclear nations to only three.

Century VI 9

To the holy temples shall be done much scandals,
That shall be accounted for honour and praises,
By one, whose medals are graven in gold and silver,
The end of it shall be in very strange torments.

To the holy temples shall be done much scandals, implies that the Exiles and Barbarians will attack people that are hiding in their Arks.

That shall be accounted for honour and praises, informs
us that the Barbarians will condone and encourage this
bad behaviour. *By one, whose medals are graven in gold
and silver,* suggests that metals of gold and silver
will be struck, honouring these attacks
on citizens within Europe.

Century VI 10

Within a little while the temple of the colours,
White and black shall be intermixed,
Red and yellow shall take away their colours,
Blood, earth, plague, famine, fire, water shall destroy them.

Within a little while the temple of the colours, or Pentagon,
will work towards victory. *White and black shall be intermixed,*
implies Caucasians will work alongside of African Americans
to achieve victory. They will be challenged by Russia and China,
or *Red and yellow.* The Pentagon will need to deal with *blood,
earth, plague, famine, fire, water,* implying, war and injury,
atmospheric changes, disease from radiation, famine, and
severe flooding caused by a rise in sea levels, as well
as rivers that have changed their course
due to nuclear explosions.

Century VI 11

The seven branches shall be reduced to three,
The eldest shall be surprised by death,
Two shall be said to kill their brothers,
The conspirators shall be killed being asleep.

The seven branches shall be reduced to three, suggests that
although Russia and China lose their nuclear arsenals during
World War 3, the seven remaining nuclear powers are further
reduced to only three. At the end of World War 3, the three
remaining nuclear powers are the United States, the United
Kingdom, and Israel. *The eldest shall be surprised by death,*
tells us that China, the oldest country, will be surprised
by death in the war. *Two shall be said to kill their brothers,*
implies two countries will be said to have killed their brother's
country and arsenal. They are South Korea which conquers
North Korea, and India and Pakistan, that exchange
missiles destroying each others arsenal.

Century VI 12

To raise an army, to ascend the Empire,
Of the Vatican, the Royal blood shall endeavour,
Flemings, English, Spain shall aspire,
And shall contend against Italy and France.

British, Dutch, and Spanish troops, still loyal to NATO
and the European Union, *shall contend against Italy and France.*
They will endeavour to take back France and Italy,
from the Exiles and the Barbarians.

Great Quatrain 131

(Century VI 21/Century VI 22/Century VI 23/Century VI 24)

Interpretation:

World War 3
Fear in the East

Summary:

When the United States achieves victory in the North Pole, then there will be fear in the East. There will be fear and trembling, in Russia and China. The Pentagon will have a new leader during World War 3, who will bring peace and stability to the world, for a very long time. A new President will be elected in the United States in 2024, just prior to World War 3, who will bear the brunt of the war. The Euro will collapse as the European currency, and the Barbarians will only accept gold, stamped leather, or the Chinese currency.

Century VI 21

When those of the Arctic Pole shall be united together,
There shall be in the East great fear and trembling,
One shall be newly elected that shall bear the brunt,
Rhodes, Constantinople shall be dyed with Barbarian blood.

When those of the Arctic Pole shall be united together, infers that when the United States achieves victory in the North Pole, then there will *be fear in the East.*

Russia and China, will be *in fear and trembling*. *One shall be newly elected,* suggests a new President of the United States will be elected in the year 2024, just prior to World War 3, who *shall bear the brunt,* of the war. At first *Rhodes and Constantinople* or Istanbul, will be attacked by Barbarians. However, eventually the *Barbarians* will be defeated, and their *blood* spilt.

Century VI 22

Within the ground of the great celestial temple,
A nephew at London by a feigned peace shall be murdered,
The boat at that time shall become schismatical,
A feigned liberty shall be with hue and cry.

Within the ground of the great celestial temple, or the Church of St. Paul in London, *a nephew* of the Royal Family will *feign a peace* with Russia, and *with hue and cry,* claim victory and *liberty.* He will promote *schism,* and ask that England break long standing relationships with other Western nations. He will *be murdered.*

Century VI 23

Despite the King, the coin will be brought lower,
The people shall rise against their King,
Peace being made, holy laws made worse,
Paris was never in such a great disorder.

Despite the King, the coin will be brought lower, implies Parisians will have no confidence in the new currency, brought in by the Barbarians.

In Europe, the Euro will collapse, because the Barbarians are refusing to accept this currency. Only gold, stamped leather, or the new Chinese currency, will be accepted. *Paris was never in such a great disorder,* states that although the French people have decided to *make peace* with the new ruler, he will still continue to violate their civil rights.

Century VI 24

Mars and the Sceptre, being conjoined together,
Under Cancer shall be a calamitous war,
A little while after a new King shall be anointed,
Who, for a long time, shall pacify the earth.

During World War 3, the *calamitous war, a new King shall be anointed,* implies that there will be a new head of the Pentagon during the war. *Who for a long time, shall pacify the earth,* explains that he will bring peace and stability to the whole world, *for a long time.*

Great Quatrain 132

(Century VI 25/Century VI 26/Century VI 27/Century VI 28)

Interpretation:

World War 3
The Great Emperor Henry
The Roman Emperor Putin

Summary:

The great emperor Henry, who is the President of the United States, will bring five major countries together to support the West, and defeat the East. This will occur when the North Pole is destroyed, and the fury of the United States Military is seen. President Putin of Russia, will enter Rome like a Roman Emperor, bringing captured NATO soldiers behind him. A new Pope from Africa, will be installed by the Russians and Barbarians.

Century VI 25

By Mars contrary shall the monarchy,
Of the great fisherman, be brought into ruinous trouble,
A young, black red shall possess himself of the hierarchy,
The traitors shall undertake it on a misty day.

Of the great fisherman, a young, black red, infers that a new Pope will be selected by Russia and the Barbarians. He will be *black,* of African descent, and he will support Russia, the red one.

By him the Vatican will be in *ruinous trouble*.
The traitors are Cardinals within the Catholic Church,
who *undertake* to elect him *on a misty day,* when
war is causing confusion.

Century VI 26

Four years he shall keep the Papal seat pretty well,
Then shall succeed one of a libidinous life,
Ravenna, Pisa, shall take Verona's part,
To raise up the Popes cross to life.

A new Pope will be elected *four years* before World War 3, in the year 2021. He shall keep *the Papal seat pretty well*, until he is killed by the Barbarians. *Then shall succeed one of a libidinous life,* indicating a new Pope from Africa, elected by Russia and the Barbarians. Both *Ravenna* and *Pisa* will help those of *Verona*, suggests *Verona* is supporting the new Pope. *To raise up the Popes cross,* infers the new Pope has a new *cross* symbol, that is very similar to the Celtic cross.

Century VI 27

In the islands from five rivers to one,
By the increase of the great emperor Henry,
By the frost of the air and the fury of one,
Six shall escape, hidden within bundles of flax.

The great emperor Henry, leader of the West, shall bring all five major countries of Europe into one, *like five rivers* into *one river*.

There will be *frost in the air*, caused by the destruction of the North Pole. Six smaller European countries will be neutral.

Century VI 28

The great Celtique shall enter into Rome,
Leading with him a great number of banished men,
The great shepherd shall put to death every man,
That was united for the Cock, near the Alps.

The great Celtique, President Putin, will lead many Exiles from Italy back *into Rome,* like a Roman Emperor. He will have captured French and NATO soldiers in chains, following behind him. They were captured *near the Alps.* These soldiers will later be executed in public, a clear war crime.

Great Quatrain 134

(Century VI 33/Century VI 34/Century VI 35/Century VI 36)

Interpretation:

World War 3
ALUS

Summary:

President Putin, will be responsible for deaths
throughout the United States, or all of the U.S., ALUS.
He will not be saved by his navy. He will be caught
between two rivers, fearing the United States Military.
In the end, he will be repentant.

Century VI 33

His last hand bloody through Alus,
Shall not save him by sea,
Between two rivers he shall fear the military hand,
The black and wrathful one shall be repentant.

His last hand bloody through Alus, suggests President
Putin of Russia will cause deaths throughout the United States,
or ALUS. *Shall not save him by sea,* predicts that his navy
will fail him. *Between two rivers he shall fear the military*
hand, infers he will be trapped between two rivers in Italy,
and *shall fear* the United States *Military.* In the end,
he shall *be repentant*, but it will be too late for that.

Century VI 34

The contraption of flying fire,
Shall trouble so much the captain of the besieged,
And within shall be so much rioting,
That the besieged shall be in despair.

The contraption of flying fire, or American air power, *shall trouble the captain* of the beseiged Barbarian army, at Milan. *And within shall be so much rioting,* that the Barbarian defenders *shall be in despair.*

Century VI 35

Near Rion and towards Blanchelaine,
Aries, Taurus, Cancer, Leo, Virgo,
Mars, Jupiter, the Sun shall burn a great plain,
Woods and cities, letters hidden in a wax candle.

Near Rion and towards Blanchelaine, in Landes, the nuclear explosion in Bordeaux will cause the sky to seem like *the sun* has come to earth.

Century VI 36

Neither good nor evil by a loud fight,
Shall reach to the borders of Perusia,
Pisa shall rebel, Florence shall be in a bad way,
A King being on his mule shall be wounded
in the darkness.

A leader of Italy, will *be wounded in the darkness,* trying to escape in an old car.

Great Quatrain 143

(Century VI 69/Century VI 70/Century VI 71/Century VI 72)

Interpretation:

World War 3
Henry the Victor

Summary:

A new President of the United States will lead
the West to victory over the East. He will have the
title of victor. President Putin of Russia will seem
to be allied with the West, before he dies. He will
say that peace should be established in Europe and around
the World, and that there should be no more war. He takes
no responsibility for World War 3, because he resigned
as President of Russia, before the war began he says.

Century VI 69

What a great pity it shall be before long,
Those that did give, shall be constrained to receive,
Naked, famished with cold, to mutiny,
To go over the mountains making great disorder.

Those who were serving with NATO Forces, are *those*
that did give. However, they are *constrained to receive*
food, because the Barbarians are using food as a weapon.
If they don't *go over the mountains making great disorder,*
then they won't receive any food, and will die.

Century VI 70

A chief of the world, the great Henry shall be,
At first, beloved, afterwards feared and dreaded,
His fame and praise shall go beyond the heaven,
And shall be contented with the title of Victor.

A new President of the United States, will be *feared* by Russia and China. He will be known by *the title Victor*, and *his fame and praise shall go beyond the heaven.* He will lead the West to victory, over the East.

Century VI 71

When they shall come to celebrate the obsequies
of the great King,
A day before he be quite dead,
He shall seem presently to be allied,
With Eagles, Lions, Crosses Crowns of Rue.

When it is clear, that President Putin will *be quite dead* the next day, and they are making arrangements for *the obsequies* or funeral, *he shall seem to be allied* with the West. He will say that peace should be established throughout the world, that there should be no more war. Also, that the new Celtic countries that formed, are truly democratic. He will admit of no responsibility for the war, because he resigned before it started, he will say.

Century VI 72

By a feigned fury of divine inspiration,
The wife of the great one shall be ravished,
Judges willing to condemn such a doctrine,
A victim shall be sacrificed to the ignorant people.

The wife of President Putin of Russia, will be attacked after his death. The *Judges* of the Barbarians, will do nothing. She *shall be sacrificed to the ignorant people,* implying the Barbarians.

113

Great Quatrain 145

(Century VI 77/Century VI 78/Century VI 79/Century VI 80)

Interpretation:

World War 3
Romans Claim Eagle

Summary:

The United States will claim victory, in the air war in World War 3. Barbarians in Germany, will take control of one of the two German NATO Fleets. A terrorist from Iran will take over Paris, and claim victory for the East. However, Switzerland and Italy, will not consent to this. Terrorists from Morocco, will enter Europe through Spain. Crescent walls from nuclear blast sites, will cause rivers to change their courses, causing flooding and drowning.

Century VI 77

By the deceitful victory of the deceived,
One of the two fleets shall revolt to the Germans,
The chief and his son murdered in their tent,
Florence, Imole, persecuted in Romania.

The Barbarians will announce *victory*, in order to *deceive* the populations of Europe. *Of the two German fleets*, one *shall revolt* to the Barbarians. *The chief German and his son, are murdered in their tent. Florence and Imole* are *persecuted* by Romanian Barbarians.

Century VI 78

They shall cry at the victory of the great Selin's crescent,
By the Romans the Eagle shall be claimed,
Ticin, Milan and Genoa consent not,
Then by themselves the great Basil shall be claimed.

Selin, a terrorist from Iran, will cause people *to cry* at his *crescent* flag, and his claims of *victory*. Russia will *claim* victory over the United States, but Switzerland and Italy will *consent not*. The United States will *claim the eagle*, infers that it will claim *victory* in the air war.

Century VI 79

Near the Tesin the inhabitants of Logre,
Garonne and Saone, Seine, Tar and Gironde,
Shall erect a promontory beyond the mountains,
Conflict given, the Po passed over, some shall be drowned.

Near the Tesin, the inhabitants of Logre, similar to *the inhabitants* near the *Garonne, Saone, Seine, Tar, and Gironde*, will experience a nuclear blast. These blasts will cause a crescent wall to be formed around the blast area, which will change the course of the rivers, causing many people to *be drowned*. When this happens in northern Italy, *the Po* River will be *passed over* by Russian troops, and *conflict* will ensue.

Century VI 80

The Kingdom of Fez shall come to Europe,
Fire and sword shall destroy their city,
The great one of Asia, by land and sea with a great army,
So that the blues, greens, crosses to death he shall drive.

Terrorists, from *the Kingdom of Fez* or Morocco,
shall come to Europe through Spain *with a great army*.
They will face the NATO *Blue* Navy, the NATO *Green*
Army, and Christians with *crosses*. President Putin
will be successful for a short period only.

Great Quatrain 150

(Century VI 97/Century VI 98/Century VI 99/Century VI 100)

Interpretation:

The 911 Attacks
Taken Captive Above Four Times

Summary:

During 911 there will be four planes taken captive above. The amphitheatre in the heavens, is where people are watching the planes above. At the instant the first plane hits the World Trade Centre tower, there is a flame. President Bush will land American troops in Afghanistan, to try to capture those responsible. The terrorists responsible, will head towards the ancient caves in the area.

Century VI 97

The heaven shall burn at five and forty degrees,
The fire shall come near the great new city,
In an instant a great flame dispersed shall burst out,
When they shall make a trial of the Normans.

In New York City, *the great new city,* there will be *fire* the instant a plane hits the tower on a *forty-five-degree* angle. At that time *the Normans*, or Americans, will be tested.

Century VI 98

Ruin shall happen to the Vandals that will be terrible,
Their great city shall be tainted, a pestilent deed,
They shall plunder sun and moon, and violate their temples,
And two rivers shall be red with running blood.

The ruin to the vandals, is the ruin to Al Qaeda. *Their city,* Kabul in Afghanistan, will be targeted, and the attacks will occur during *the sun and moon,* or day and at night. *The two rivers* of New York, the Hudson, and the East River, will run *red with blood* from the destruction of the twin towers.

Century VI 99

The learned enemy shall go back confounded,
A great camp shall be sick and in effect through ambush,
The Pyrenean Mountains shall refuse him,
Near the rivers discovering the ancient hives.

The learned enemy are the terrorists who study the Koran. There camp will *be sick* and ineffective, because of *Am-bush*, or because of American President George W. Bush. American troops will land near the mountains in Afghanistan, to cut off that path. *Near the rivers, discovering ancient hives,* refers to the honeycomb of caves that exist in this region, where the terrorists hope to hide.

Century VI 100

Daughter of Laura, sanctuary of the sick,
Where to the heavens is seen the amphitheatre,
A prodigy being seen, the danger is near,
Thou shall be taken captive above four times.

Daughter of Laura, infers that President Bush's wife Laura Bush, will visit the *sanctuary of the sick,* or hospitals of the sick and wounded from 911. The *amphitheatre in the heavens,* tells us that there are events taking place in the sky worth watching. Everyone is watching the sky clear of planes. *A prodigy being seen, the danger is near,* refers to Mohamed Atta, who was a prodigy of Osama Bin Laden, and represented a clear threat. *Thou shall be taken captive above four times,* is an eerie reference, to the fact that four planes will be captured, or hijacked above.

Great Quatrain 186

(Century VIII 41/Century VIII 42/Century VIII 43/
Century VIII 44)

Interpretation:

World War 3
A Fox

Summary:

President Putin of Russia, called a fox, will claim
to be a public saint, when he is elected by the Barbarians
without saying a word. Afterwards, he will tyrannize suddenly,
the NATO leader in Europe. The nine nuclear nations will
be reduced to seven, as both Russia and China will lose
their nuclear arsenals. The United States will control
space and airspace, during World War 3.

Century VIII 41

A fox shall be elected that said nothing,
Making a public saint, living with barley bread,
Shall tyrannize after upon a sudden,
And put his foot upon the throat of the greatest.

A fox shall be elected that said nothing, tells us that
President Putin of Russia, claiming to be a public saint,
will be elected by the Exiles and Barbarians without saying
anything. After which he *shall tyrannize suddenly, and put*
his foot upon the throat of the NATO leader in Europe.

Century VIII 42

By avarice, and force and violence,
Shall come to vex his own chief of Orleans,
Near St. Memire, assault and resistance,
Dead in his tent, they shall say he sleepeth there.

By avarice, and force and violence, President Putin
will come to worry *his own chief of Orleans,* the
Exile leader at Orleans, near Paris. Near St. Memire
and Padua, President Putin will be *dead in his*
tent. They shall say he sleepeth there,
afterwards.

Century VIII 43

By the decision of two things bastards,
Nephew of the blood shall occupy the government,
Within Lector shall be blows of darts,
Nephew through fear shall fold up his ensigns.

Two distant relatives with Napoleonic blood,
will *occupy the government* of France for the Exiles,
at first. *Within Lector shall be blows of darts,* suggests
that Moldavia will be targeted by NATO from the air.
This will cause the Russian leader, to *fold*
up his ensigns.

Century VIII 44

The natural begotten of Ogmion,
From seven to nine shall be put out of the way,
To king of long, and friend to half man,
Ought to Navarre prostate the fort of Pau.

The natural begotten of Ogmion, from seven to nine shall be put out of the way, tells us that the leader of NATO, Ogmion, will see the nine nuclear powers reduced to seven nations. Russia, and China, will lose their nuclear weapons arsenals. *To king of long, and friend to half man,* suggests that the United States will control all space and airspace, in World War 3. *Half man,* represents high altitude aircraft for the United States. NATO will attack the Barbarians, in Navarre at *the fort of Pau.*

Great Quatrain 203

(Century IX 9/Century IX 10/Century IX 11/Century IX 12)

Interpretation:

World War 3
New Clay

Summary:

The Exiles and Barbarians will look for new clay. People that they can shape to their cause. They will be motivated by gold and silver. Children in France, will be forced to drink the poisonous water in the blast crater, as there is no other water near at hand. The Barbarians will have Judges, that will put people to death wrongfully. These will be public executions.

Century IX 9

When a lamp burning with an unquenchable fire,
Shall be found in the Temple of the Vestals,
A child shall be found, water running through a sieve,
Nismes to perish by water, the city hall shall fall at Toulouse.

The *burning with an unquenchable fire,* will *be found in the Temple of the Vestals,* infers that there is a fire that never goes out. This is the fire from a nuclear explosion in Southern France. The fire is under the water, in the large crater formed when Marseille was destroyed.

The water is the Mediterranean Sea, which has come
far inland in France, as a result of the explosion. *Nismes,*
in Southern France, is now under this large lake. Children
will be forced to drink this poisonous water, as there
is no other water supply near by. *The city hall at
Toulouse,* will also *fall* into the *water.*

Century IX 10

*Monk and Nun having exposed a dead child,
To be killed by a bear and be carried away by a glazier,
The camp shall be pitched at Foix and Panniers,
Against Toulouse, Carcassonne shall be against them.*

A *Monk and Nun that* are working for the Russians,
will help to expose French children to the Russian Bear,
which will cause them to be carried away with the Exiles.
The Exiles will pitch a tent, *at Foix and Panniers,* and
they shall be *against Toulouse and Carcassonne.*

Century IX 11

*The just shall be put to death wrongfully,
Publicly, and being taken out of the midst,
So great a plague, shall break into that place,
That the judges shall be compelled to run away.*

Rough justice, by the Exiles and Barbarians, will
cause *the Just,* to *be put to death wrongfully.* However,
the radiation in these areas, will be so severe, that even
the Barbarian *Judges shall be compelled to run away.*

Century IX 12

The so much silver of Diana and Mercury,
The statutes shall be found in the lake,
The potter seeking for a new clay,
He and his, shall be filled with gold.

Those that follow the idols of *silver,* will find that the silver was placed *in the lake* to hide it during the invasion into France. The Exiles, will look *for a new clay,* or new supporters. People that they can shape to their cause, using gold, instead of silver. *He and his, shall be filled with gold,* suggests President Putin of Russia and the Barbarians, will be motivated by gold.

Great Quatrain 207

(Century IX 25/Century IX 26/Century IX 27/Century IX 28)

Interpretation:

World War 3
The Great Cap

Summary:

The great cap, or Russian Pope, will ask that certain Italian provinces be assigned to him, as Papal states. He will be given Voltri and Piombino, along the Italian coast. Both areas will experience the wind from nuclear explosions, with radiation poisoning. Bridges will need to be constructed by both sides, during World War 3.

Century IX 25

Going over the bridge, to come near the rose-trees,
Arriving late, much sooner than he thought,
Shall come the news of Spaniards to Beziers,
Who shall chase this hunting undertaking.

The Barbarians moving north of Paris will come *over the bridge, near the rose-trees,* at the town of Rosiers in Limousin. Arriving late, they will hear news of NATO Spanish troops going *to Beziers.* They will be chased by these troops.

Century IX 26

A foolish going out, caused by sharp letters,
The great cap shall give what is not his,
Near Vultry by the walls of green capers,
About Piombino the wind shall be in good earnest.

The newly elected Pope from Russia, *the great cap,* will *cause sharp letters* to be sent, asking for the Papal states to be assigned to him. He will be given *Voltri,* and *Piombino.*

Century IX 27

The fence being of wood, close wind, bridge shall
be broken,
He that is received high, shall strike at the Dauphin,
The old Teccon shall pass over smooth wood,
Going to the right on the side of the Duke.

Although the old wooden *bridge shall be broken* in Italy, by NATO, the Barbarians in Italy simply construct their own bridge from wood, and pass over.

Century IX 28

Symaclian Sail, Massillon port,
In Venice to march toward the Hungarians,
To go away from the Gulf and Illyrian Straits,
Toward Sicily, the Genoese, with cannon shots.

After the explosion in the *Massillon port,* or port of Marseille, the NATO Army in Venice will move toward Hungary, and toward Sicily with cannon shots.

Great Quatrain 208

(Century IX 29/Century IX 30/Century IX 31/Century IX 32)

Interpretation:

World War 3
Column of Porphyry

Summary:

A column of porphyry, or nuclear blast cloud, will be seen in Israel, at Lod. There will be an earthquake following the blast. The United States will avenge this attack on Israel, which comes from a Russian nuclear submarine in the Black Sea. With this attack, the Middle East will erupt in war again. President Putin of Russia will appear to resign as President of Russia, just prior to World War 3. However, he remains President, and goes with the Barbarians and Russian troops into Europe.

Century IX 29

When he that giveth place to nobody,
Shall forsake the place taken and not taken,
Fire, ship, by bloody bitumen at Charlieu,
Then St. Quentin and Calais shall be taken.

President Putin of Russia, shall *forsake the place taken, and not taken,* implies that President Putin will appear to resign, but doesn't.

Then there will be a *ship* sunk, with *fire and blood,* mixed with *bitumen* oil. This refers to the American aircraft carrier sunk just prior to the beginning of World War 3. Then NATO will secure Northern France and Belgium, at *St. Quentin and Calais.*

Century IX 30

At the harbour of Puola and St. Nicolas,
A Norman ship shall perish in the Frantic Gulf,
At the Cape of Byzantia, the streets shall cry "Alas!",
Help from Cadiz and from the Spanish King.

A Norman ship shall perish in the frantic gulf, infers that an American aircraft carrier is sunk in the Aegean Sea. *At the Cape of Byzantia, the streets shall cry "Alas!",* implies that in Istanbul, there will be some who *shall cry alas,* as an expression of grief. Help from British NATO ships, at *Cadiz* and Gibraltar, will be sent right away.

Century IX 31

There shall be an earthquake by mortars,
Cassich, St. George shall be half swallowed up,
The war shall awake the sleeping peace,
On Easter Day, shall be a great hole sunk in the temple.

On Sunday April 5th, 2025, *Easter Day*, there will be a nuclear explosion at Lod Israel, near Tel Aviv. This will cause a small earthquake. It will come from a Russian nuclear submarine in the Black Sea.

The sleeping peace, or in other words the Middle East, *shall awake in war.* There will *be a great hole,* where once there was a *Temple,* or Synagogue.

Century IX 32

A deep column of fine Porphyry shall be found,
Under whose base shall be important writings,
Bones, hairs twisted, Roman force tried,
A fleet about the port of Methelin.

Everyone will be able to see *the column of Porphyry,* or mushroom cloud from the blast. *Roman force tried,* states that the nuclear attack on Israel, will be avenged by the United States. A NATO Fleet at *the Port of Methelin* or Mytilene Lesbos, will put to sea immediately.

Great Quatrain 223

(Century IX 89/Century IX 90/Century IX 91/Century IX 92)

Interpretation:

World War 3
The Young Ogmion

Summary:

The young Ogmion, or NATO leader in Europe,
will replace the older Ogmion who is killed trying
to keep the Barbarians out of Europe. A leader
of Germany, will ask for help from the Barbarians
in Hungary. He will use this pretext of asking for help,
as a method to invite the Barbarians into Germany.
Biological weapons will be introduced into parts
of the Ukraine and Greece, by the Russians.

Century IX 89

Seven years of prosperous fortune shall Philip have,
And shall beat down the attempt of the Barbarians,
Then in his heyday, perplexed with misdirections,
Young Ogmion shall pull down his strength.

For seven years of prosperous fortune, shall the
older Ogmion *Philip have. And shall beat down the attempt*
of the Barbarians, infers he shall have some success
in stopping *the Barbarians.*

However, as World War 3 unfolds, he is *perplexed* as the
leader of NATO in Europe, because of *misdirection's by* the
Barbarians. This *perplexity,* will cost him his life. The *young
Ogmion,* will then enter, and succeed where
the older one failed.

Century IX 90

A Captain of great Germany,
Shall come to yield himself by simulating help,
To the King of Kings, with the help of Hungary,
So that his revolt shall cause great bloodshed.

A captain of great Germany, in World War 3, will
ask for help from the leader of the Barbarians, that have
entered into *Hungary*. This request for help is only *simulated
help,* not real. *Hungary,* now under the control of the Barbarians,
will say that they can help Germany. This approach of having
the Barbarians invited into Germany, was contrived long ago.
However, it leads to *a revolt* within *Germany,* because many
Germans want NATO Forces to control Germany,
not Russia. There is sharp fighting,
and *great bloodshed.*

Century IX 91

The horrid pestilence shall be in Corinth and Nicopol,
The Crimeans and the Macedonians also,
It shall waste Thessaly and Amphipolis,
An unknown evil and the refusal of Anthony.

Biological weapons, *the horrid pestilence,* are
introduced by the Barbarians, into *Crimea as well
as Macedonia. It shall waste Thessaly and Amphipolis,*
and leave whole populations dead or infected. This *evil*
will not be withdrawn, because President Putin of Russia,
also called the great *Anthony,* will *refuse.*

Century IX 92

*The King shall desire to enter into the New City,
With foes they shall come to overcome it,
The prisoner being freed, shall speak and act falsely,
The King being gotten out, shall keep far from enemies.*

A Barbarian leader, or *king, shall desire to enter*
Nuremberg, Germany, *the New City.* He will release
a German leader who was a *prisoner.* However, this German
leader will *speak and act falsely,* because he is under pressure
to say what the Barbarians wanted him to say. Once released,
he will *keep far from his enemies,* not wanting
to be captured again.

Great Quatrain 227

(Century X 5/Century X 6/Century X 7/Century X 8)

Interpretation:

World War 3
Deucalion Again

Summary:

The Gardon River at Nismes will overflow when
its course has changed from the nuclear explosion
at Rouen. Those that will look toward the blast sight,
will think they are seeing Deucalion again, as there
is massive flooding everywhere. In the rural areas
of Washington State, a Russian missile will hit.
There will be three Russian missile hits on the
United States, within seven days in May,
during World War 3.

Century X 5

Albi and Castres shall make a new league,
Nine Aryans, Lisbon and Portuguese,
Carcassonne, Toulouse, shall make an end
of their confederacy,
When the new chief shall come from Lauragais.

In South Eastern France, near *Albi and Castres, nine Aryans,* or nine Iranian terrorists, coming from *Lisbon and* the *Portuguese,* will enter Southern France. They will be captured by a new chief, the new NATO leader in France.

Century X 6

Gardon at Nismes, waters shall overflow so high,
That they think Deucalion be born again,
Most of them will run into the colossus,
And a sepulchre, and fire extinguished, shall appear.

The *Gardon* River *at Nismes,* will *overflow* when its course has been changed by the nuclear blast at Rouen. While some people will run away from the flood, *most of them will run* toward the flood, trying to see what has happened. They will *think Deucalion is born again,* and the world is flooding. They shall see the *fire extinguished,* from Rouen at a distance, and they shall think to have seen *a sepulchre* or burial chamber, where before was fertile farm land.

Century X 7

A great war is in preparation at Nancy,
The Aemathien shall say, submit to all, to me,
The British Isle shall be put in want for salt and wine,
The two bloody friends shall keep Metz long.

NATO Forces are *preparing for war at Nancy,* France. The chief of the Barbarian group will say, *submit all to me. The British Isles* will be *in want* for imported goods, which have been interrupted because of the war. French and British troops, *the two bloody friends,* will meet near *Metz,* to form a resistance.

Century X 8

Index and Poulse shall break the forehead,
Of the son of the Earl of Senegal,
The Myrnamee by many at a full bout,
Three within seven days shall be wounded to death.

Between the towns of *Index* and *Palouse,*
in Washington State, a Russian missile will hit the
rural area causing a nuclear explosion. A distant relative
of William Pitt, *Earl of Senegal,* will be injured by the attack.
However, those loyal to him will see *three wounded to death
in seven days. The three,* are three missiles that will strike
the United States, during the exchange of missiles
with Russia and China. This will occur *within
seven days* in May.

Great Quatrain 231

(Century X 21/Century X 22/Century X 23/Century X 24)

Interpretation:

World War 3
A Barrel of Honey

Summary:

A captured Barbarian leader from Italy, will save
himself from death, by promising NATO Forces
a barrel of honey, or in other words, information.

Century X 21

To spite the King, who took the part of the weaker,
He shall be murdered, presenting the jewels,
The father and the son going to vex the nobility,
It shall be done to them as the Magi did at Persia.

The King of Sardinia, because he *took the part of the weaker,*
and spared lives, will *be murdered, presenting the jewels.*
He will be murdered by the Barbarians that he came with,
even as he presents all the wealth of Sardinia to them.

Century X 22

For not consenting to the divorce,
Which afterwards shall be acknowledged unworthy,
The King of the Island shall be expelled by force,
And another subrogated, who shall have no
mark of the King.

The King of Corsica, *for not consenting to the
divorce,* to which everyone *acknowledged as unworthy,*
will *be expelled* by Barbarians and *another* substituted.

Century X 23

*The remonstrances being made to ingrates,
At the time the army shall seize Antibes,
In the vault of Monaco, they shall make their complaints,
And at Frejus both of them shall take their share.*

At the time the army shall seize Antibes, infers that
the Barbarian army from Italy will move through *Monaco,
Antibes,* and Nice. The King of Monaco will hide in a secret
chamber or *vault,* below the city. *In the vault of Monaco,
they shall make their complaints,* implies he will
hear all the complaints of his citizens.

Century X 24

*The captured prince captured in Italy,
Shall pass by sea through Genoa to Marseilles,
By great efforts of foreign forces overcome,
A barrel of honey shall save him from fire.*

The prince captured in Italy, will work for the Barbarians.
He will pass through Genoa, going toward Marseille.
By great efforts of foreign forces overcome, predicts that
 NATO troops will overcome the Barbarians. *A barrel
of honey shall save him from fire,* states that he will
save himself from being killed,
by promising information.

Great Quatrain 236

(Century X 41/Century X 42/Century X 43/Century X 44)

Interpretation:

World War 3
Shadow of the Seven

Summary:

As each city and province is liberated by NATO,
the shadow of the seven nuclear explosions, that occurred
simultaneously in May, is like a spectre. People want those
responsible, to face the death penalty. At first the Exiles aren't
viewed as a threat. However, given time people will understand
that they have an agenda that is both political and military.

Century X 41

On the borders of Caussade and Charlus,
Not far from the bottom of the valley,
Of Ville Franche shall be heard the music of lutes,
Great dancing and company of people met together.

In Southern France, at *the bottom of a valley,* there will
be partying and *music of lutes,* as some people celebrate the
return of the Exiles. *Great dancing and company of people
met together,* implies that at first, the Exiles aren't seen
as a real threat. However, with time people will see that
the Exiles have an agenda, which is civilian,
political, and military.

Century X 42

The humane reign of an angelic offspring,
Shall cause his reign to be in peace and union,
Shall make war, captive shutting it half up,
He shall cause them to keep peace a great while.

A new President of the United States, will at first *reign in peace and union*. However, as he is forced to *make war*, he will defeat both Russia and China, and keep them *shut half up*. He will force them *to keep peace a great while*, make changes, and bring in democracy and civil rights.

Century X 43

The time too good, too much of royal bounty,
Feats and prompt defeats, quick negligence,
Fickle shall believe false of his loyal spouse,
He shall be put to death for his benevolence.

The French leader at the time of the Exiles, will be *too good* and have experienced *too much of royal bounty*. He will be unprepared for what lies ahead. He will have *prompt defeats*, and *quick negligence*. He will not believe there is any harm from the returning Exiles, even though his loyal wife warns him to the opposite. When he is captured, *he shall be put to death for his benevolence*. The Exiles and Barbarians, will execute him in public.

Century X 44

At the time that a King shall be against his own,
One born at Blois shall subdue the Ligurians,
Mammel, Cordova, and the Dalmatians,
Shadow of the seven, both a Royal present and spectre.

When the Exiles and Barbarians are in retreat in Italy, *one born in Blois,* with NATO, *shall subdue* them in North Western Italy and South Eastern France. As each city, town, and province is liberated from the Barbarians, the *shadow of the seven* nuclear explosions that occurred in May, is present like a *spectre* or ghost. People want those responsible, to face the death penalty.

141

Great Quatrain 242

(Century X 65/Century X 66/Century X 67/Century X 68)

Interpretation:

World War 3
An Earthquake in May

Summary:

An earthquake in May 2025, will occur between
Russia and the United States. This will involve
an exchange of missiles, between the countries.
The internet and communication will be out from May,
until the end of August. The United Kingdom will
work with the United States, to establish security
around the world.

Century X 65

O mighty Rome, thy ruin approaches,
Not of thy walls, but of thy blood and substance,
The sharp by letters, shall make so horrid a notch,
Sharp iron thrust in all the way to the shaft.

O mighty Rome, thy ruin approaches, states that Rome
will be ruined by the influx of Exiles and Barbarians. The ruin
is not of the buildings, but *of thy blood and substance,* implying
the people of Rome. Although there is a nuclear explosion
at the mouth of the Tiber River, Rome is not destroyed.

The sharp by letters, shall make so horrid a notch, infers the Barbarians will put up notices to the public, regarding the changes they want.

Century X 66

The chief of London by rule of America,
The Island of Scotland shall be tempered by Frost,
Kings and Priests shall have one, who is a false Anti-Christ,
Who will put them together in discord.

The chief of London by rule of America, indicates that the Prime Minister of England, working with the United States, will establish security across the British Isles and the world. *The Island of Scotland shall be tempered by frost,* tells us that in Scotland, a group of Politicians has decided to declare Scottish independence, with help from Russia. However, this will be declared illegal, and the Scottish people will reject this. *Kings and Priests shall have one, who is a false Anti-Christ,* implies the leaders of these independent splinter countries, together with the new Pope from Russia, will be under the control of Russia and President Putin.

Century X 67

The earthquake shall be so great in the month of May,
Saturn, Caper, Jupiter, Mercury in Taurus,
Venus also, Cancer, Mars in Zero,
Then shall hail fall bigger than an egg.

The earthquake shall be so great in the month of May, implies total war, between the United States and Russia, will occur in May, with an exchange of missiles. In that time, the internet and communication will be offline, from May until the end of August. *Then shall hail fall bigger than an egg.* The West will experience very cold weather in the summer, with very large hail caused by the destruction of the North Pole. People must get under cover during this hail, as it is deadly to those caught in the open.

Century X 68

The marines shall stand before the city,
Then shall go away for a little,
A citizen army shall then hold the ground,
The fleet returning and recovering a great deal.

The marines shall stand before the city, predicts that the United States will send in Marines to help Venice. However, they shall leave for a short while, before returning. *A citizen army shall then hold the ground* against the Barbarians, and the United States *Fleet* will *return,* after establishing security in the seas and oceans of the world.

Great Quatrain 243

(Century X 69/Century X 70/Century X 71/Century X 72)

Interpretation:

President Putin
666 is the Number of a Man

Summary:

President George W. Bush will take decisive action on 911, and attack the terrorists responsible around the world. The sight of planes flying into towers, will not be easily forgotten by people around the world. The one that planned the 911 attack, will be arrested at Reggio Emilia in Italy. President Putin will be promoted to Prime Minister, and then President of Russia in 1999. He will be the one directly responsible for terrorists using Mini-subs with nuclear weapons, and for the nuclear attacks on the United States, Europe, and the West.

Century X 69

The bright action of the new old exalted,
Shall be so great throughout the North and South,
By his own sister great forces shall be raised,
Fleeing, murdered near the bush of Ambellon.

The bright action of the new old exalted, refers to President
George W. Bush newly elected, as opposed to his father
President George Bush Senior. President George W. Bush's
immediate action was clear and decisive following 911,
so that those in both the north and south of the world,
understood that the war on terrorism would not be easy,
and would not be short term. *By his own sister great forces
shall be raised,* implies that the United Kingdom will also raise
military forces to help out. *Fleeing, murdered near the bush
of Ambellon,* states that President George W. Bush will attack
the terrorists, wherever they are, and that the United States
is like the Am-Bellon, or American *Bellon,* wife of Mars,
the god of war. What Nostradamus means by this,
is that the Statue of Liberty, is going to war.

Century X 70

The eye of the object shall make such an excrescence,
Because so much, and so burning shall fall the snow,
The field watered shall come to decay,
That the primat shall succumb at Reggio.

The eye of the object shall make such an excrescence,
refers to the sight of planes on 911 being flown into towers.
This will make such a sight, that people will not easily forget
the image. *Because so much, and so burning shall fall the snow,*
states that the burning and dust will fall like snow. *The field
watered shall come to decay,* is the field where United
Airlines Flight 93 crashed, which was reclaimed land
from an old mine, not intended for crops. It was
destined to be a monument.

The one that *shall succumb at Reggio,* is the one responsible
for the organizing of the attack. Mohamed Daki was arrested
in 2003 at *Reggio* Emilia, in Italy, for his part in planning
the 911 Attacks.

Century X 71

The earth and the air shall freeze with so much water,
When they shall come to worship Thursday,
That which shall be, never was so fair,
From the four parts, they shall come to honour him.

The Russian leaders who *come to worship Thursday,*
are those that have chosen Wednesday May 7th 2025,
as the day that Russia will attack the United States and Canada
with nuclear weapons. They worship Thursday, the day after
the attacks, when they hope the United States is destroyed. When
this attack occurs, it will have repercussions *from the four parts*
of the world. *The earth and the air shall freeze with so much*
water, infers that the destruction of the North Pole will change
the atmosphere, causing freezing rain and cold during late
spring and early summer. *They shall come to honour him,*
 implies the United States will be successful,
and that the President of the United States
and the Pentagon leaders will
be honoured afterwards.

Century X 72

In the year 1999 and seven months,
From the sky shall come an alarmingly powerful King,
To raise again the great King of the Jacquerie,
Before and after, Mars shall reign at will.

In the year 1999 and seven months, the President of Russia, Boris Yeltsin, appointed Vladimir Putin to the position of Prime Minister of Russia. This is the first major step of Putin's political career. In December 1999 of the same year, Yeltsin appointed Putin as President of Russia. *The year 1999,* is a particularly fateful time for the world. Here we see the number 666, as clearly belonging to the Russian President. With President Putin of Russia, World War 3 will eventually occur, as he will be the direct cause of terrorists using Mini-subs with nuclear weapons, and the subsequent nuclear war with the West.

Great Quatrain 249

(Century X 93/Century X 94/Century X 95/Century X 96)

Interpretation:

World War 3
A and A

Summary:

America, A and A, will defeat both Russia and China.

Century X 93

The new ship shall make a voyage,
Into the place, and thereby transfer the empire,
Beaucaire, Arles, shall keep the hostages,
Near them shall be found the two columns of porphyry.

The new ship, that shall change *the Empire* of the European Union, is the Russian mini-sub, which will cause the destruction of major European Ports. As a result, those of Arles and Beaucaire, will keep some Barbarians hostage, that are responsible for two nuclear explosions near there.

Century X 94

From Nismes, from Arles, and Vienna contempt,
They shall not obey the Spanish proclamation,
To the laboratories to condemn the great one,
Six escaped in a spherical habit.

The new Barbarian countries in Spain, will issue
a *proclamation* to France and Europe, to surrender
to the Russian Barbarian forces. *France and Vienna,*
will be in *contempt* of *the Spanish proclamation.* The Russians
will deny that they have anything to do with the nuclear
explosions. They will say that this type of nuclear material doesn't
exist in Russia, and that the only country to carry this radioactive
material is Iran. As a result, countries around the world
will go back *to the laboratories.*

Century X 95

A most potent King shall come into Spain,
Who by sea and land shall subjugate the south,
This evil shall beat down the horns of the crescent,
And lower the wings of those of Friday.

A most potent King shall come into Spain, states
that a Christian NATO leader will go into Southern Spain,
and *subjugate the south.*

Century X 96

Religion of the name of the seas shall come,
Against the Sect of Caitiffs of the Moon,
The deplorably obstinate sect shall be afraid,
Of the two wounded by A and A.

Terrorists will *be afraid,* after both Russia and China
are defeated by the United States. *Wounded by*
A and A, implies they are wounded by America.

Great Quatrain 250

(Century X 97/Century X 98/Century X 99/Century X 100)

Interpretation:

World War 3
Manna Shall No More Fall

Summary:

Manna shall no more fall, tells us that after World
War 3, a Great Famine will follow. This famine will
affect the animals of the world, just as much as humans.
The food chain will be destroyed, and large greenhouses,
will need to be constructed, as the soil of the earth will
be contaminated with radiation. The Great Empire
of the United States and England will last
for more than three hundred years.

Century X 97

The Triremes full of captives of all ages,
Time good and evil, the sweet for the bitter,
Prey to the Barbarians, they shall not be too hasty,
Desirous to see the feather complain to the wind.

The Barbarians are making slaves of people, as they move
through Europe. Slaves, or *captives of all ages,* people exposed
to their evil. While they shall be preyed on by the Barbarians,
this will change, and eventually the reverse will happen.

When this happens, the people of Europe will be *desirous to see the feather complain to the wind,* implying they will desire to see them complain, when they face the death penalty at the International Criminal Court, at The Hague.

Century X 98

The clear splendour of the joyous maid,
Shall shine no more, she shall be a great time without salt,
With merchants, ruffians, wolves odious,
All promiscuously, she shall see a universal monster.

When the Barbarians are moving through Europe, *the clear splendour of the joyous maid,* is set upon by *merchants, ruffians and odious wolves. All promiscuously, she shall see a universal monster,* tells us that she will need the protection of good people, during these evil times.

Century X 99

At last the wolf, the lion, ox and ass,
The gentle doe, shall lie down with mastiffs,
The manna shall no more fall to them,
There shall be no more watching and keeping of mastiffs.

At last the wolf, the lion, ox and ass, the gentle doe, shall lie down with mastiffs, explains that there is a worldwide famine following World War 3. This famine affects the animals of the world, just as much as humans. The animals lying down beside each other, are starving to death, and too weak to hunt.

The manna shall no more fall to them, implies that
food will not come easily or quickly again, either for
animals or humans. People will not *keep mastiffs,* or pets,
as they can't provide the food, and during the Great Famine,
pets are vulnerable to attack by humans,
as a food source.

Century X 100

The great empire shall be in England,
The Pempotan for more than three hundred years,
Great armies shall pass through land and sea,
The Lusitanian's shall not be content therewith.

The great empire will be in the United States and England,
which will last *more than three hundred years,* as the most
powerful. The Allies will pass through Europe, and into
Southern Spain, to eject the Barbarians. The Barbarians
will *not be content,* as they are finally challenged,
destroyed, and removed from Europe.

Great Quatrains and World War 2 with Symbolism

Great Quatrain 8

(Century I 31/Century I 32/Century I 33/Century 34)

Interpretation:

World War 2
A Bridge Too Far

Summary:

The Arnhem Bridge, or a bridge too far, will not be taken by Allied paratroopers. Nostradamus predicts that the wars in France, will stretch over hundreds of years. He states that England will lose its great Empire after World War 1, and that Churchill will come forward before World War 2.

Century I 31

So many years the wars shall last in France,
Beyond the course of the Castilian monarch,
An uncertain victory three great ones shall crown,
The Eagle, the Cock, the Moon, the Lion leaving
the sun in its mark.

So many years the wars shall last in France, tells us that the wars in France will last over many centuries. *Beyond the course of the Castilian monarch.* The Castilian monarchy lasted 500 years, and Nostradamus predicts the wars in France will last over a similar period.

After World War 1, *an uncertain victory three great ones shall crown, the eagle, the cock, the moon, the lion.* The three great ones, the United States, France, and Great Britain, will have an uncertain victory after World War 1. This uncertain victory will lead to World War 2, says Nostradamus. *Leaving the sun in its mark*, states that Japan would be relatively unaffected by World War 1.

Century I 32

The great Empire shall soon be translated,
Which shall grow soon into an inferior place of small
account,
In the middle of which he shall come,
To lay down his sceptre.

The great Empire shall soon be translated, states that there will be a great change for Great Britain after World War 1. *Which shall grow soon into an inferior place of small account*, implies that after World War 1, Great Britain will lose its Empire and become smaller as a world power. *In the middle of which he shall come, to lay down his sceptre*, informs us that Churchill will come forward to reach power in Britain.

Century I 33

At a great bridge, near a spacious plain,
The great Lion by Caesarius forces,
Shall come to be pulled down before the
rigorous city,
The gates which shall be shut to him.

At the great bridge, near a spacious plain,
refers to the bridge at Arnhem, in the flat country
of the Netherlands, and Operation Garden Market.
The Arnhem bridge was a bridge too far.
*The great lion, by Caesarius forces, shall come
to be pulled down before the rigorous city,* implies
that General Montgomery, the lion, will not be able
to capture the bridge, due to its rigorous defence
by the Germans. *The gates shall be shut to him,*
implies the paratroopers will
be overrun at Arnhem.

Century I 34

The bird of prey flying to the window,
Before the battle shall appear to the French,
One shall take good omen of it,
the other, an ambiguous one,
The weaker party shall hold it a good sign.

*A bird of prey flying to the window, before battle
shall appear to the French,* explains that the French
and Dutch citizens will see the British and American
paratroopers in their windows, coming to the ground.
*One shall take it as a good omen of it, the other an
ambiguous one, the weaker party shall hold it a good sign.*
This tells us that while the French and Dutch citizens
hold this to be a good sign for the end of the war,
the French Resistance movement is uncertain as
to whether the paratroops can succeed. The weaker
party are the Germans, who see it as a good sign
because the paratroopers are easy to attack.

Great Quatrain 13

(Century I 51/Century I 52/Century I 53/Century 54)

Interpretation:

World War 2
Events Leading Up

Summary:

Events leading up to World War 2, are covered here. After World War 1, war will return to France and Italy. German tanks will perfect the pincer movement. Hitler will cause the dismemberment of Europe, and his race laws will trouble all Christianity. His swastika will be inclined to Russia, and two equal forces on either side of Germany will bring it down.

Century I 51

Heads of Aries, Jupiter and Saturn,
O Eternal God, What changes there shall be,
After an era, his evil returns,
Gaul and Italy, what commotion.

Here we see the *return of evil* times and war again, after World War 1. *Gaul and Italy, what commotion,* states that France and Italy will go through enormous changes during World War 2.

Century I 52

The two evils of Scorpion being joined,
The Grand Seignior murdered in his hall,
Plague to a Church by a king joined to it,
Europe in the depths and dismembered.

The two evils of the scorpion being joined is describing the pincer movement of the German tanks, which they perfected during World War 2. *The Grand Seignior murdered in his hall*, refers to President Hindenburg, whom Nostradamus states was murdered by Hitler on his death bed in 1933. Indeed, Hitler was one of the last persons to see President Hindenburg alive. *Plague to the church by a king joined to it,* implies that the Nazi church, will be a plague, with Hitler as leader. *Europe in the depths and dismembered*, is telling us that Hitler will cause the dismemberment of Europe, precipitating crisis upon crisis.

Century I 53

Alas how a great people shall be tormented,
And the Holy Laws in total ruin,
By other laws, all Christianity troubled,
When new mines of gold and silver will be found.

Alas, how a great people shall be tormented, and the holy laws in total ruin, refers to the Jewish Community, a great people, and the holy laws in ruin because of a lack of ethics by Nazi Germany. *By other laws, all Christianity troubled*, tells us about anti-Semitic laws.

When new mines of gold and silver will be found, suggests that the Jewish Community will move, go to North America, and find new ways to make gold and silver.

Century I 54

Two revolts shall be made by the evil torch bearer,
Which shall make a change of the reign and age,
The mobile sign to the right shall meddle,
And shall have an inclination to the two equals.

Two revolts shall be made by the evil torch bearer, refers to the first revolt Hitler led in Bavaria, which ended in failure, and the second revolt where he took over the government of Germany in 1933. *Which shall make a change of the reign and age,* reveals that the second revolt will cause a change in the peace and stability of Europe.

The mobile sign to right shall meddle, is stating that the swastika, the symbol of the Nazi's, will go to the right or towards Russia. *And shall have an inclination to the two equals*, implies that Germany will have two equal forces against it, namely the United States and Britain on the one side, and Russia on the other side.

Great Quatrain 45

(Century II 77/Century II 78/Century II 79/
Century II 80)

Interpretation:

World War 2
War Crimes

Summary:

The war crimes of World War 2, include the Warsaw Ghetto Uprising, German U-Boats, and the Warsaw Uprising of the Polish Army. In the Warsaw Ghetto Uprising, the Jewish community had only primitive weapons to defend themselves. The German U-Boats, called the concealed evil, attacked slow moving civilian ships. Finally, the Warsaw Uprising of the Polish army, against the Germans was declared a war crime.
The Russians later arrested and executed
all Polish citizens involved.

Century II 77

Being repulsed with bows, fires and pitch,
Cries and howlings shall be heard about midnight,
They shall get in through the broken walls,
The betrayers shall run away through the sewers.

In the Warsaw Ghetto Uprising, the Jewish community had only primitive weapons to defend themselves. These included *bows, fire and pitch.*

Some of the leaders of the Warsaw Ghetto Uprising escaped, *through the sewers*. This was a war crime, against a civilian population.

Century II 78

The great Neptune, in the deep of the sea,
Having joined African and French blood,
The islands shall be put to the sword and the slow rowing,
Shall do them more harm than the concealed evil.

In World War 2, German submarines used bases in *France and Africa*. The German U-Boats, called by Nostradamus *the concealed evil*, would often attack *the slow*-moving ships, regardless of whether they were civilian or military.
The islands were the British Isles that were dependant for their survival on the American convoys.

Century II 79

The frizzled and black beard by fighting,
Shall overcome the fierce and cruel nation,
The great Henry shall free from bonds,
All the captives made by Selim's banner.

Nostradamus describes Turkey as *the fierce and cruel nation*.

Century II 80

After the battle, the eloquence of the wounded man,
Within a little while shall procure a holy rest,
The great ones shall not be delivered,
But shall be left to their enemies will.

The Warsaw Uprising of the Polish Army in August 1944 was a major war crime. Soviet forces under Stalin, refused to help the Polish army against the Germans, even though they were only a few miles away. Despite pleas by Churchill and Roosevelt, their requests were ignored by Stalin.

The great ones of the Warsaw Uprising, were later *left to their enemies will,* inferring that those who survived would be arrested, tried and executed by the Russians. On the 60th anniversary of this war crime against the Polish people in 2004, the delegation included the German Chancellor, the United Kingdom Deputy Prime Minister, Representatives from the United States, and Pope John Paul II.
Russia sent no delegation.

Great Quatrain 50

(Century II 97/Century II 98/Century II 99/
Century II 100)

Interpretation:

World War 2
D-Day Augurs

Summary:

The D-Day Augurs are the weathermen that predict the strong north wind on the day of the invasion. The assault of the Germans on England, causes many to seek the shelter of the great line, in the tube or subway. Hitler will have the blood of his victims from the Holocaust on his face, implying that he is held responsible. Japan's declaration of war on Britain, will cause Hitler to be overconfident.

Century II 97

Roman Pontiff take heed to come near,
To the city watered with two rivers,
Thou shall spit there thy blood,
Thou and thine when the rose shall bloom.

Pope Pius XII, served from 1939 until 1958. During World War 2 he failed to say anything against the Holocaust, for which he was much criticized. In 1954 he became ill, and died in 1958 after a long illness. After his death, the Roman Catholic Church had a rebirth.

Century II 98

He that shall have his face bloody,
With the blood of the victims near to be sacrificed,
The sun coming into Leo shall be an augury by presage,
That then he shall be put to death for his confidence.

He that has his *face bloody with the blood of his victims* is Hitler, who was responsible for the Holocaust. *The sun coming into Leo*, suggests that Japan will declare war on Great Britain during World War 2, causing Hitler to be overconfident. This overconfidence, is a foreshadowing of his death to come.

Century II 99

The Roman country in which the augur did interpret,
Shall be too much vexed by the French nation,
But the Celtic nation shall fear the hour,
The North Wind had driven the navy too far.

The Augurs or weathermen, predicted a strong *north wind* on D-Day. The strong *north wind* caused the invasion to be delayed for 24 hours, worrying those looking to invade the *French nation*. On the day of invasion, June 6th, the wind was so strong that it blew *the navy too far* east of the intended positions.

Century II 100

In the islands shall be such horrible tumults,
That nothing shall be heard by a warlike surprise,
So great shall be the assault of the robbers,
That everyone shall shelter himself under
the great line.

In World War 2 *nothing is heard by warlike surprise*, since the British had radar, and had broken the German cipher machine. Everyone in London sheltered themselves in the subway or tube, where possible. This is *the great line* that Nostradamus refers to.

Great Quatrain 59

(Century III 33/Century III 34/Century III 35/Century III 36)

Interpretation:

World War 2
Hitler's Brain Stroke

Summary:

Hitler will have a brain stroke, when he has no more troops.
The German army is predicted to go to Paris. During World
War 2 many people will go to the Alps, to find safety.
When Japan is in decline, Germany will soon be defeated
by Russia. Russia shifts resources to the western front
from the east, and Germany has made no plans
for this contingency.

Century III 33

In the city where the wolf shall go,
Near the place the enemies shall be,
An army of strangers shall spoil a great country,
The friends shall go over the mountains of the Alps.

The city where the wolf or German army goes,
is Paris. This is *near the place where the enemies shall be,*
or the Allies will eventually land, along the northern coast
of France. The *army of strangers who spoil a great country,*
is the German army. *Friends* of France leave for Switzerland,
and *go over the mountains,* to the Alps for protection.

Century III 34

When the eclipse of the sun shall be,
At noon day, the monster shall be seen,
It shall be interpreted other ways,
Then for a dearth, because nobody hath
provided for it.

When Japan is in *the eclipse*, or decline, then Russia, *the monster shall be seen*. Russia will move all its eastern divisions to the western front, shifting the war in their favour. Then the Russian army will take the offensive against the Germans, and the German army will be unprepared for this wave of new units against them, *because nobody hath provided for it.*

Century III 35

Out of the deepest part of the West of Europe,
From poor people a young child shall be born,
Who with his tongue shall seduce many people,
His fame shall increase in the Eastern Kingdom.

Hitler will arise in western Europe and *seduce many people,* with his tongue. *From poor people a young child shall be born,* states that he came from a humble beginning. At first the German troops are considered liberators in eastern Europe, however this attitude changes quickly.

Century III 36

One burned, not dead, but apoplectical,
Shall be found to have eaten up his hands,
When the city shall damn the heretical man,
Who as they thought had changed their laws.

Hitler is *burned* by the Russians on the eastern front, and *apoplectical,* or has a brain stroke as a result. Berlin will eventually condemn Hitler, who as they thought *had changed their laws* for his own benefit. He will be found to *have eaten up his hands*, suggests that he has spent all his troops, and has no more to send.

Great Quatrain 87

(Century IV 45/Century IV 46/Century IV 47/Century IV 48)

Interpretation:

World War 2
Hornets Flying Low

Summary:

Northern France will see the sky darkened
by many Allied aircraft that resemble hornets
flying low. Their wings are painted with hornet stripes,
so that their aircraft are not confused with the enemy
aircraft. The battle of Dunkirk will see British troops
trapped, and surrounded on the beaches of Dunkirk.
The Germans will go no further, and through
the miracle of foggy weather the British
will escape. The fact defended excellently
well, is the Maginot Line.

Century IV 45

By a battle a King shall forsake his kingdom,
The great commander shall fail in time of need,
They shall be killed and routed few shall escape,
They shall be cut off; one only shall be left for a witness.

At the start of the battle of Dunkirk, *the great commander* or supreme allied commander French General Gamelin, failed the Allied forces in their *time of need*.

As a result, the British forces were *cut off* on the
beaches of Dunkirk, and only through the miracle
at Dunkirk were they able to escape. The British forces
that formed the perimeter around Dunkirk were captured.
What followed was a war crime. The German SS Division
that captured the 97 British troops, in the town of Le Paradis,
massacred them. *They shall be cut off; one only shall be left
for a witness.* One soldier survived to tell their story after
the war, at the Nuremburg trials. The officer
in command of the SS Division
was executed in 1949.

Century IV 46

The fact shall be defended excellently well,
Tours beware of thy approaching ruin,
London and Nantes by Rheims shall stand upon their
defence,
Do not go further in foggy weather.

The fact defended excellently well, was the French Maginot
Line, which was intended to defend against a German attack,
at the start of World War 2. However, the Germans simply
moved north of the line, by-passing it completely. *Tours*
became the temporary city for the French government
in June 1940. *Tours beware of thy approaching ruin.*
The Germans used incendiary bombs on Tours, which
caused a huge fire and destroyed most of the city
as predicted. British forces were deployed in northern
France, and were *upon their defence* at Dunkirk. Only
by a miracle of *foggy weather*, and poor planning
by the Germans, were the British forces able
to escape at Dunkirk.

Century IV 47

The wild black one, after he shall have tried,
His bloody hand by fire, sword bended bows,
All the people shall be so frightened,
To see the greatest hanged by neck and feet.

The wild black one, Mussolini, after leading Italy into a losing war on the side of the Axis powers, was captured by partisans in northern Italy and executed along with other fascist leaders. He was later hung on meat hooks upside down by *the feet*, so *all the people shall be so frightened,* that they would be discouraged from fighting.

Century IV 48

The plain about Bordeaux fruitful and spacious,
Shall produce so many hornets and so many grasshoppers,
That the light of the sun shall be darkened,
They shall fly so low; a great plague shall come from them.

The plain around northern France, *fruitful and spacious, shall produce so many hornets and so many grasshoppers,* describes Allied aircraft on D-Day. In order that there was no confusion, between their own aircraft and enemy aircraft, all Allied aircraft were painted with the peculiar *hornet* strips on their wings. There were so many aircraft, some flying *very low, that the light of the sun shall be darkened* for a period of time. They were *a great plague*, and trouble to the Germans as predicted.

Great Quatrain 111

(Century V 41/Century V 42/Century V 43/Century V 44)

Interpretation:

World War 2
The Double Army

Summary:

Hitler will have a double army, namely the regular
German army, and then the SS troops. He will feign anger,
to invade Poland and Czechoslovakia. Mussolini will try
to renew the golden age of Rome, only to produce
a brass image. The Holocaust will start along
the Rhine and in Mainz.

Century V 41

Being born in the shadows and nocturnal time,
He shall be sovereign in kingdom and bounty,
He shall cause his blood to be born again from
the antique urn,
Renewing a golden age instead of a brass one.

Mussolini, *born in the shadows*, will become the
first fascist leader of Italy, and Prime Minister in 1922.
He hopes to make Italy like ancient Rome, powerful,
trying to renew *a golden age* for the country. Instead,
he only creates *a brass* image of the golden age.

Century V 42

Mars being raised to its highest watchtower,
Shall cause the Allobrox to retreat from France,
The people of Lombardy shall be in so great fear,
Of those of the eagle, comprehended under Libra.

Once in power, Mussolini begins by making war against France *the Allobrox,* in 1940, only to meet stiff resistance. With casualties high, Italy retreats, with their only gain a small town on the coast. This incursion was overshadowed by Germany's invasion of France, which raised war *to its highest watchtower,* and caused *the Allobrox to retreat.* The people of *Lombardy* will *be in great fear* of American troops, the eagle, at the end of the war.

Century V 43

The great ruin of the sacred things is not far off,
Provence, Naples, Sicily, Sez and Ponce,
In Germany towards the Rhine and Cologne,
They shall be vexed to death by those of Moguntia.

The great ruin of the sacred things is not far off, implies the Jews of Italy will soon be rounded up and sent to concentration camps. Beside the Jews of the *Rhine and Cologne,* there is concern over the Jews of Moguntia, or Mainz, Germany. The Jews of Mainz, a very old community dating to the 10th century, were helped by an Italian family by the name of Kalonymos. This family was crucial, in assisting the Yeshiva Centre for Talmudic studies.

Century V 44

By sea the red one shall be taken by pirates,
The peace by that means shall be troubled,
He shall commit anger by a feigned act,
The high priest shall have a double army.

The red one taken by pirates, refers to the initial gains of Germany in World War 2. After Germany, *the pirates*, broke its pact with Russia and attacked Russia in June 1941, they made some initial gains. However, *peace* between Germany and Russia, would remain *troubled*. Hitler, *feigning anger* with Poland and Czechoslovakia, used this anger as an excuse to invade both countries. Hitler, the *high priest*, had *a double army*, namely the regular German army, and the SS troops.

Great Quatrain 135

(Century VI 37/Century VI 38/Century VI 39/Century VI 40)

Interpretation:

World War 2
The Holocaust

Summary:

The Holocaust will begin with the arrest of the leaders
of the Jewish Communities along the Rhine, like Mainz,
and Cologne. Anne Franks ancestors came from this area,
dating back to 1462. She was more German than the Nazi's.
The guilty SS troops responsible for the Holocaust,
will hide among the German population after the war.

Century VI 37

The ancient work shall be finished,
From the house tops shall fall great misfortunes,
The innocent in fact, shall be accused after his death,
The guilt shall be hidden in a wood in misty weather.

The ancient work shall be finished, implies that the
battlements built along the Atlantic coast by Hitler,
to stop an invasion from the Allies, will be completed.

The guilt shall be hidden in a wood in misty weather, explains that the guilty SS troops, responsible for the Holocaust, will try to hide among the German population, in the open, after the war.

Century VI 38

To the vanquished the enemies of peace,
After they shall have overcome Italy,
A bloody Black One shall be committed,
Fire and blood shall be discharged, and water coloured with blood.

To the vanquished the enemies of peace, tells us Germany, *the vanquished,* will make war not peace. At the end of the war, Germany will take over Italy or *overcome Italy. A bloody black one,* inferring Mussolini, will *be committed,*
to continuing the war.

Century VI 39

The child of the kingdom through his father's imprisonment,
Shall be deprived of his kingdom for the delivering of his father,
Near the Lake Trasimene shall be taken in a tower,
The troop that was in hostage being drunk.

The child of the kingdom through his father's imprisonment, states that Hitler came from a family, where his father kept his family virtually prisoners. Hitler will *be deprived of his kingdom,* or Germany, for *delivering his father,* or fatherland, to the enemy.

The Germans were holding a line against the Allies, at *Lake Trasimene* during World War 2, and were forced back to the Gothic line. Some German and Italian troops, are *taken in a tower, near Lake Trasimene.*

Century VI 40

The great one of Mayence to quench a great thirst,
Shall be deprived of his high dignity,
Those of Cologne shall mourn him so much,
That the Great Groppe shall be thrown into the Rhine.

The great one of Mayence, or Mainz, was the leader of the Jewish Community along the Rhine. He was taken at the time of the Holocaust, and *mourned by those of Cologne.* This was very close to Frankfurt, where Anne Franks ancestors came from, dating back to 1462. Anne was more German than the Nazi's. *That the great Groppe shall be thrown into the Rhine,* refers to the ultimate downfall of Hitler.

Great Quatrain 148

(Century VI 89/Century VI 90/Century VI 91/Century VI 92)

Interpretation:

World War 2
Midway
The Stinking and Abominable Defiling

Summary:

Admiral Nagumo is in a quandary, as he tries to decide between two different courses of action for his Aircraft carriers at Midway. He was driven mad by American Aircraft that sink four Japanese Aircraft carriers. The reason that they were sunk, was because the Japanese were treacherous cup bearers the year before, with an attack on Pearl Harbour. With Admiral Nagumo's failure at Midway, Yamamoto becomes the new architect of Imperial Japan.

Century VI 89

Between two boats one shall be tied hand and foot,
His face anointed with honey, and be nourished with milk,
Wasps and bees shall make much of him mad,
For being treacherous cup bearers and poisoning the cup.

Between two boats, tied hand and foot, refers to the Japanese Admiral Nagumo, who on June 4th 1942, is in a quandary, as tries to decide between two different courses of action.

Needless to say, he wasn't able to make the necessary changes to prevent the sinking of four Aircraft carriers, which were like *honey* to a bee. He was driven *mad by the wasps and bees,* of American Aircraft. This was caused, because the Japanese were *treacherous cup bearers, poisoning the cup*, suggesting that the defeat at Midway was caused by the treachery of Pearl Harbour on December 7th 1941, the year before.

Century VI 90

The stinking and abominable defiling,
After the deed shall be successful,
The great one excused for not being favourable,
That Neptune might be persuaded to peace.

The stinking and abominable defiling, which was *successful,* was Pearl Harbour. *The great one excused,* was Admiral Yamamoto, who was against the strike, but later came to approve it. He had hoped that after the attack, the United States would *be persuaded to peace.* Instead, because the official note to the United States, explaining the breaking of diplomatic relations was late, it served to strengthen America's resolve, not weaken it.

Century VI 91

The leader of the Naval War,
Red, rash, severe, horrible executioner,
Being slave, shall escape, hidden among the harness,
When shall be born to the great one, a son named Agrippa.

The leader of the naval war for Japan, was Admiral Nagumo, who also suffered from *severe, red rashes,* from arthritis. At Midway he escapes off of his aircraft carrier to another ship, *hidden among the harness.* With his failure at Midway, Yamamoto becomes the new *Agrippa*, or architect of Imperial Japan.

Century VI 92

A Princess of exquisite beauty,
Shall be brought to the chief, the second fact betrayed,
The city shall be given to fire and sword,
By too great a murder, the chief man of the King
shall be hated.

At the time that the *chief* of the Japanese Imperial force is marrying *a Princess of beauty,* Tokyo is bombed by the United States in the Doolittle raid. *The city was given to fire,* since many of the houses were of wood. The Doolittle Raid caused those leading Japan, to be shocked at how vulnerable Japan was, and the leader of the Japanese Military was subsequently *hated.*

Great Quatrain 190

(Century VIII 57/Century VIII 58/Century VIII 59/
Century VIII 60)

Interpretation:

World War 2
Twice Setup High

Summary:

Germany will be twice setup high, and twice
brought down, in World War 1 and World War 2.
Both the Eastern and Western fronts in Germany will
weaken. Hitler will rise from a common soldier in World
War 1, to head of the Supreme Command in World War 2.
General Charles De Gaulle, will relocate his French
government back to France in the middle of the night.

Century VIII 57

*From a simple soldier, he shall come to have
supreme command,
From a short gown he shall come to a long one,
Valiant in arms, no worse man in the church,
He shall vex the priests, as water does a sponge.*

In World War 2, Hitler came from *a simple soldier*
in World War 1, to head of the *Supreme Command*.

From a short gown to a long one, suggests that at first,
he wasn't taken seriously, and was viewed as a rabble-rouser.
Valiant in arms, refers to his receiving the Iron Cross
1st and 2nd Class in World War 1. However,
he is the *worst in the church,* annoying *the
priests* because of his lack of humanity.

Century VIII 58

*A kingdom in dispute and divided between the brothers,
To take the arms and the Britannic name,
And the English title, he shall advise himself late,
Surprised in the night and carried into the French air.*

The kingdom in dispute is France, which during World
War 2 is *divided* between Vichy France, and Free France.
The one with the *English title,* is General Charles
De Gaulle, who is leader of the French government in exile.
He *surprises* the British by relocating his government back
to France *at night.* He flew into *French air* space,
eight days after D-Day, and he *advised* the British
late, as predicted.

Century VIII 59

*Twice set up high, and twice brought down,
The East also the West shall weaken,
His adversary after many fights,
Expelled by sea, shall fail in need.*

Twice set up high, and twice brought down, refers
to Germany during the first and second world wars.

The east also the west shall weaken,
predicts that both the Eastern and the Western
Fronts, will weaken because of Germany's adversaries.
Eventually Germany will be *expelled by sea,* indicating
its ports will become blockaded by the British Royal Navy.
At that time, Germany *shall fail.*

Century VIII 60

The first in France, the first in Romania,
By sea and land to the English and Paris,
Wonderful deeds by that great company,
By ravishing, Terax shall ruin Norlaris.

The first in France, and *the first in Romania,*
refers to Hitler and Germany in World War 2.
The English and Americans with the French,
by sea and land, will do *wonderful deeds,* with
their *great company* of large forces. They shall
ravish the German industrial base, and the
ports for their submarines.

Great Quatrain 195

(Century VIII 77/Century VIII 78/Century VIII 79/ Century VIII 80)

Interpretation:

World War 2
The Anti-Christ

Summary:

Hitler is the Anti-Christ, who will be brought to nothing. His war will last 27 years, from 1918 to 1945. He will be responsible for destroying his fatherland, and for killing many innocent people. People will remain silent, hoping to survive.

Century VIII 77

By Anti-Christ, three shall be brought to nothing,
His war shall last seven and twenty years,
The heretics dead, prisoners exiled,
Blood, human body, water made red, earth shrunk.

Hitler is the *Anti-Christ,* and the *three brought to nothing,* are Himmler, Goering, and Goebbels. His war *shall last 27 years,* from the end of World War 1 to the end of World War 2. *The heretics dead* or *prisoners exiled,* are the SS followers.

At the end of World War 2, after the carnage,
the *earth will shrink* due to technological advances.

Century VIII 78

A Bragamas with his harmful tongue,
Shall come to break the God's sanctuary,
He shall open the gates to heretics,
By raising the militant church.

The *Bragamas* or bragger, is Hitler, *with his harmful tongue.* He shall come *to break God's sanctuary,* attack the Synagogues and *raise a militant church,* of *heretics.*

Century VIII 79

He who by iron shall destroy his father, born
in Nonnaire,
Shall in the end carry the blood of the gorgon,
Shall in a strange country make all so silent,
That he shall burn himself, and his double talk.

He who by iron shall destroy his father, predicts that Hitler will destroy his fatherland, Germany. Hitler shall *carry the blood of the gorgon,* suggests he will turn people to stone, with his atrocities.

Century VIII 80

The blood of the innocent widow and virgin,
Much evil committed by the means of that great rogue,
Holy images, dipped in burning wax candles,
For fear, nobody shall be seen to stir.

Hitler will be responsible for the death *of innocent* people, and *commit much evil.* Due to *fear,* people will be silent.

Great Quatrain 248

(Century X 89/Century X 90/Century X 91/Century X 92)

Interpretation:

World War 2
Ropes of Rushes

Summary:

The Holocaust is described, as a tangle of ropes
in rushes. Himmler's death by suicide, is predicted.

Century X 89

The walls shall be turned from brick into marble,
There shall be peace for seven and fifty years,
Joy to mankind, the aqueduct shall be rebuilt,
Health, abundance of fruits, joys and a mellifluous time.

There shall be peace for seven and fifty years,
predicts a period of peace and prosperity for 57 years,
following the end of World War 2. At which time the
911 Attacks begin, eventually leading to World War 3.

Century X 90

The inhuman tyrant shall die a hundred times,
In his place shall be put a savant a kindly disposed
man,
All the senate shall be at his command,
He shall be angry by a rich malicious person.

The inhuman tyrant is Hitler. After his death, Admiral
Donitz is chosen by Hitler to take over Germany.
He is perceived by most people to be *a kindly
disposed man,* even though he is given
a sentence of 10 years for war crimes.

Century X 91

*The Roman clergy in the year 1609,
In the beginning of the year, shall make a choice,
Of gray and black, come out of the country,
Such a one never a worse was.*

If we add the Council of Nicea to *1609,* we have
the year 1934, when Hitler had just come to power.
He starts to set up concentration camps, and the *Roman*
Catholic *Clergy* makes the decision not to criticize Hitler.
The black and gray are the German army and the SS
uniforms of World War 2. *Never a worse* one,
refers to Hitler.

Century X 92

*The child shall be killed before the fathers' eyes,
The father shall enter into ropes of rushes,
The people of Geneva shall not ably stir themselves,
The chief lying in the middle like a log.*

The child shall be killed before the fathers' eyes,
implies the Holocaust, and its impact
on Jewish families.

Fathers and their families *shall enter into ropes
of rushes,* inferring they are caught up in a tangle
of destruction. The death by suicide of Heinrich
Himmler, *like a log in the middle*
of the room, is predicted.

Great Quatrains and World War 1 with Symbolism

Great Quatrain 23

(Century I 91/Century I 92/Century I 93/Century 94)

Interpretation:

World War 1
The Great War

Summary:

Nostradamus calls World War 1, the Great War. World War I began as a series of alliances, giving the impression that the gods started the war. War will be seen in the air, for the first time. The affliction of war will be greater on the left, or the western side. World War 1 will be the first war that has significant civilian deaths, despite the denials by the Germans. Turkey will join the Axis powers,
and women's rights in Turkey will
be protected by the law.

Century I 91

The Gods shall make it appear to mankind,
That they are the authors of a great war,
The sky that was serene shall show sword and lance,
On the left hand the affliction shall be greater.

The Gods shall make it appear to mankind, that they are the authors of a great war, implying that the *great war* to end all wars, will begin as a series of alliances and mobilizations.

This gave the impression that the gods had started the war, and that there was no particular incidence responsible. Nostradamus calls World War 1 the *great war.* *The sky that was serene shall show sword and lance,* tells us that for the first time, airplanes will be used during World War 1. On the left hand, meaning on the western front, *the affliction* of war will *be greater.*

Century I 92

Under one shall be peace, and everywhere clemency, But not for a long while, then shall be plundering and rebellion, By a denial shall town, land and sea be assaulted, Dead and taken prisoner shall be the third part of a million.

Under one shall be peace, and everywhere clemency, but not for a long while, then shall be plundering and rebellion, suggests that President Woodrow Wilson, will at first try to seek a peaceful resolution to the war. However, when it became clear that Germany was going to continue plundering American merchant ships, the United States declared war.

*By a denial shall town, land, and sea be assaulted,
dead and taken prisoner shall be a third part
of a million,* states that the First World War,
will be the first war that will cause significant
civilian deaths, despite the denials
by the Germans.

Century I 93

*The Italian land of the mountains shall tremble,
The Lion and the Cock shall not agree very well,
And for fear shall help one another,
Only Spain and the Celts shall be neutral.*

*The Lion and the Cock shall not agree very well
together, and for fear shall help one another,* indicates
that even though France and England didn't work
well together in World War 1, they kept the
Alliance going out of fear of its failure.

The Italian land of the mountains shall tremble,
describes how Italy would be induced to join the Allies,
and attack the Austrian Hungarian Empire from the
mountains. Spain and the Celts in the Iberian
Peninsula, *shall be neutral.*

Century I 94

*In the port, Selim the tyrant shall be put to death,
And yet, liberty shall not be recovered,
The new War by vengeance and remorse begun,
A lady by force of fear shall be honoured*

The 1913 Sublime Porte Incidence, which was a *coup d'état* in the Ottoman Empire of modern-day Turkey, had the result of improving secular laws for education and women's rights. Women's rights were henceforth protected, by *fear* of the law, which helped Turkish society move forward.

The new war by vengeance begun, occurred when Turkey entered World War 1, on the side of the Axis powers.

Great Quatrain 25

(Century I 99/Century I 100)

Interpretation:

World War 1
The Gray Bird

Summary:

Sir Edward Grey, the gray bird, will offer an
olive branch of peace to Germany. This will come
about after the great one, Francis Joseph, Austria's Emperor
dies. Imperial Russia will keep friendship with England
and France in World War 1. After many battles the
low birth rate in France, will leave many small
towns like Narbonne virtually empty.

Century I 99

Le Grand Monarque shall keep company,
With two kings united in friendship,
Oh, what fights shall be made by their followers,
Children, O what a pity about Narbonne.

The *Monarch* of Imperial Russia keeps *friendship*
with England and France during World War 1. After
many large battles and many men lost, the low birth
rate in France will leave many small towns
like *Narbonne* virtually empty.

Century I 100

For a long while shall be seen in the air a gray bird,
Near Dola and the Tuscan land,
Holding in his beak a green bough,
Then a great one shall die and the war be finished.

A gray bird, holding *a green bough*, is Sir Edward Grey, Great Britain's Foreign Secretary in 1916. During World War 1, he held out an olive branch of peace for Germany. Known as the House-Grey memorandum of fall 1916, it stated that if Germany rejected President Wilson's mediation, then the United States would enter the war against Germany. Then in November 1916, the *great one* Francis Joseph, Austria's old Emperor died, which set into motion a whole new round of peace negotiations, leading to the end of the war.

Glossary of Symbols

A

Ancient Ones -	Japan
Anti-Christ -	Hitler
Angel -	Woman
Arethusa -	God of Water, or Firemen
Androgen Born -	Hydrogen bomb
Augur -	Weatherman or Pope.
Ancient Work -	German Defences in France on D-Day
Anvil in a Ball -	Hydrogen bomb in a strange design
Aquitanian England -	The South Western corner of France
Ambellon -	America and the Goddess of War
Antipodes -	At the other end of the world
Alpha and Alpha -	A and A, or America

B

Barn on the Sea -	Aircraft Carrier
Beast Speaks -	Hydrogen Bomb Explosion
Bird of Prey -	Paratroopers or U.S.
Barbarous Odour -	Biological Weapons
Brazen Beard -	Terrorist
Bows, Fires, and Pitch -	Ancient Weapons
Branches -	Royal Family
Bells Ringing -	Sirens and Church Bells to Warn People
Bragamus -	Hitler the Braggart
Bichoro -	Old French word for Victory
Barrel of Honey -	Information

C

Chief One -	The President of Russia
Cock -	France
Concealed Evil -	German U-Boats
Celts -	Exiles or Barbarians
City of the Sun -	Heliopolis or Baalbek
Captain of Germany -	Hitler
City of Plancus -	Lyons
Celtic Leader -	Exile Leader
Citizens Mesopotamia -	Citizens of Southern France
Crosses Topsy-Turvy -	Swastika
Chariot -	Tank or Armoured Car

D

Darts -	Mini-subs
Divine sickness -	Diabetes
Dissembling -	Hiding under pretence
Dart of Heaven -	Missile

E

Emperor -	Napoleon
Eagle -	The United States or Louis XIII
Empire -	Russia or the European Union
English Prince Mars -	Prince Charles
English King -	King Charles
Eastern Wall -	China
Evil Torch Bearer -	Hitler
Eye of Ravenna -	Evil Psychic Bin Laden

F

Fishing Boat -	Christianity
Fish that is Terrestrial -	Amphibious Vehicles
Fish like a Loon -	Mini-sub with a strange design
Fleur de Lys -	France
Flying Fire -	Attack Aircraft
Fox -	President of Russia

G

Great Venice -	European Union
Geneva -	The United Nations or Geneva
Great Line -	The London Subway or Tube
Great Troubled Cloak -	Mao Zedong
Great War -	World War 1
Great Lion -	UK or General Montgomery
Great Mountain-	Chinese Economy
Gaul -	France
Great Famine -	Famine on a Large Scale
Grand Seignior -	President Hindenburg
Great Henry -	The Western leader
Great Dame -	Queen Elizabeth
Great Luminaries -	Sun and Moon
Great Mountain –	Chinese Economy
Great Solyman -	Israel
Great Tuscan -	Napoleon
Great Empire -	European Union
Great Jovialist -	President Obama
Great Anthony -	President Putin
Great Duke -	President Putin
Great Lutheran -	German or General Blucher
Great Allobroges -	Exiles call Themselves
Great Pilot -	Prince William
Great Pouch -	President Putin
Garden of the World -	New Jersey

H

Hog Half Man -	Fighter Pilot
Harness -	Protection
Half Hog -	British Bulldog
Holy Temples -	Places of Safety
Holy Widow -	Queen Elizabeth II
Holy Empire -	Celtic Countries

I

Iron -	Tanks
Iron Fish -	Submarine

L

Lion or Leopard -	United Kingdom
Lion heart -	Terrorist leader
Libyan Tribe -	Terrorist Followers
L'Isle -	ISIL
Leo -	Astrological Sign
Lame One -	President Roosevelt
Lamp of Trajan -	Lighthouse at Tiber River.

M

Moon -	Moon, or China
Mars -	War
Mobile Sign -	Swastika
Monarch -	King, Leader, or Terrorist
Movement with feet -	Fascism
Melite -	Citizen of Malta
Mabus -	Military Leader in Europe
Macedonia -	Greeks or the West
Maritime City -	London

Masculine Woman -   Premiere of China
Magnanimous Act -   American Citizenship for France
Militant Church -   National Socialism
Magna Vaqua -   The opposite of Magna Carta
Medusian Design -   Plans of President Putin

N

Normans -   The U.S. or the U.K.
Noble Romans -   The Democracies
New City -   Nuremberg or New York
New Old One -   Churchill
No Direction -   No Responsibility
New Sect of Philosophers -   Fascists or Communists

O

Old Olestant -   Stalin

P

Persia -   Iran
Phoenix -   Napoleon
Postulant One -   Edgar Cayce - American Psychic
Plague -   Disease or Radiation Sickness
Poles -   The North and South Poles
Pricks and Bites -   Moral Issues
Pau, Nay, Loron -   Napoleon
Place of Half Language -   Place of Half Truths
People of a New Leven -   People that want Civil Rights
Pellex -   Concubine
Phocens -   People of Marseille

Q

Quadrangle -	Louvre or Tennis Court

R

Romans -	The U.S. or UK
Red One -	Russia
Red Reds -	Red Guards in the 1960's
Republic -	United States or France
Rose of the World -	The Jewish Community in Greece, The Delphi Oracle
Royal Infant -	Prince George
Rude Prancing Horse -	Painting of Napoleon Crossing the Alps
Royal Prelate Bowing -	Japan and Leader of Japan
Recloning -	Cloning or Recloning
Ropes of Rushes -	Holocaust

S

Sun -	Sun, Japan or Louis XIV
Sects -	Political or Philosophical Divisions
Shaven Heads -	Marines or Navy Seals
Serpents in the Air -	Russian Aircraft
Strange Ship -	Mini-sub
Sceptre -	Political or military Power
Subrogate Exancle -	Substitute female helper
Schismatic -	Divided
Scourge -	War
Saturn -	Planet of Trade and Commerce
Swarm of Bees -	Attack Aircraft or Paparazzi
Ship of Mole -	Ship carrying Russian Troops
Slavic Nation -	Russia
Salic Law -	Daughters cannot inherit
Stinking -	Pearl Harbour

Shackles -   Slavery

T

Three Lions -	India or Iraq
Temple of Colours -	Military Headquarters
Translated -	Changed or Different
Two Heads and Four Arms -	Joint Russian Chinese Military
Two Nephews -	Two Admirals of the U.S. Navy
Three Hundred -	Exile and Barbarian leaders
Twelve Red One's -	The Terrorists recruited by Russia
Trident -	Power over the Oceans
Trojan Blood -	Untrustworthy
Three Harlots -	Russia, China, and Iran.

U

Underneath the Cord -	Parachute with Nuclear Bomb
Unhappy Republic -	France
Upon a Horse -	In or on a Boat or Ship
Utopia -	What the Exiles are trying to sell

V

Victorious Vanquished -	Germany
Vexed -	Worried
Venus -	Princess Diana

W

White and Red -	The United States
Wild Boar -	Germany
Wild Black One -	Mussolini
Wild Name -	President Obama
Wild One -	President Putin
White Clay -	Radioactive material
Wrestlers -	Putin and Chinese Premier

www.ingramcontent.com/pod-product-compliance
Lightning Source LLC
Chambersburg PA
CBHW052349220526

45465CB00003BA/1033